TINDERBOX HEROES

CONTENTS

FOREWORD

As the chair of the committee set up to organise the commemoration of the 50th anniversary of the Cheapside Street Disaster I am delighted to introduce you to Tinderbox Heroes.

Publication of this dramatic and moving book is one of the events marking that terrible day on the 28th of March 1960 when 14 firemen and five Salvage Corps members died in a whisky bond explosion in Glasgow. Planning for the anniversary began in 2008 when the Board of Strathclyde Fire & Rescue, of which I am a vice convener, and Chief Officer Brian Sweeney pledged that this occasion would not pass unnoticed.

The committee includes Assistant Chief Officer Lewis Ramsay of Strathclyde Fire & Rescue, the authors of Tinderbox Heroes, and two retired fire service members who were in attendance at Cheapside Street, Joe Smith and Bill Wilson. Sadly we lost a committee member, Enoch Humphries, former president of the Fire Brigades Union, who passed away last year.

Other events to mark Cheapside Street included a service in Glasgow Cathedral, a ceremony at the Cheapside Memorial at the Necropolis overlooking the cathedral and the unveiling of a plaque to be placed on the Clyde Walkway near the scene of the disaster.

Also, pupils from the primary schools closest to Cheapside Street – Anderston and St Patrick's – took part in a project to create a commemorative mosaic. The youngsters chatted with retired firefighters and sat in a vintage fire engine – something that would have delighted me as a boy!

As a Glasgow City Councillor who is proud of his city, Tinderbox Heroes reminds us of an important period in Glasgow's history – the Tinderbox City era of devastating fires. If, like me, you are of a certain age, you will remember many of these events. If, however, you are slightly younger, you will also be touched and inspired by the accounts of courage, grit and determination shown the Fire Service members of that time.

Before you immerse yourself in Tinderbox Heroes, might I suggest you do your bit for today's firefighters and check that your home has working smoke detectors and that you ask your local Fire and Rescue Service to carry out a free home fire safety visit?

Thank you

Councillor Tommy Morrison

CALL THE FIRE BRIGADE AT ONCE

DON'T ASSUME SOMEONE ELSE HAS DONE SO

Even if you think you have extinguished a fire, the Fire Brigade should be called in, as hidden smouldering may continue.

Make sure that all members of your household know the position of the nearest fire alarm or telephone—and how to call the Fire Brigade.

THE SERVICES OF THE FIRE BRIGADE ARE FREE

LIVING IN THE TINDERBOX

Why did Glasgow become known as the Tinderbox City?

The title may have been thought up by some postwar newspaper headline writer, but it stuck. Other large British cities had their major fires, of course, but Scotland's largest city grabbed most of the attention.

A series of fires running from the late 1940s and through the '50s, '60s and into the '70s destroyed property and lives on a terrible scale. Fires such as the blaze which destroyed the Arnott Simpson's department store in 1951 erased major landmarks from the cityscape.

If anyone in Britain or even abroad wanted to quote an example of a fire that claimed a horrendous number of lives, they only had to turn to Glasgow. There was, for instance, the James Watt Street fire that killed 22 furniture factory workers in 1968. Then there was the Cheapside Street Disaster of 1960 and the Kilbirnie Street fire of 1972 which together claimed the lives of 26 Fire Service personnel.

What was it about Glasgow that seemed to make it an unusually fertile ground for fire?

James Smith, a co-author of this book who was a member of Glasgow Fire Service through most of this period and has a deep knowledge of the city's fires and fire services, argues that Glasgow was, in a way, a victim of her Victorian architectural heritage.

Compared to English cities such as London or Coventry, Glasgow suffered very little bomb damage during the Second World War. Whereas photographs of neighbouring Clydebank after its two-night Blitz in March 1941 reveal scenes of utter devastation, Glasgow came through the war virtually untouched.

Glasgow had an outstanding legacy of 19th Century buildings that prompted the poet laureate and architectural campaigner John Betjeman to describe her as Britain's finest Victorian city. There was a down-side to this, however.

Smith states: "German bombers had that bit farther to fly to attack Glasgow so they concentrated on the major industrial cities south of the Border. As a result Glasgow still had old industrial buildings remaining beside her dockland that would have been largely destroyed elsewhere.

"The large cubic capacity of properties had caused concern since Victorian times. There were warehouses like vast storage caverns which were so big that sprinkler systems, if there were any, couldn't do their job if a fire broke out."

Glasgow's Firemaster, Martin Chadwick, touched on this issue in an article in his 1958 annual report entitled "Why the Increased Fire Losses in Industry etc?". Chadwick pointed out that by far the greatest proportion of Glasgow's industrial and commercial buildings were not built or designed for their current purpose. Many of these buildings had "serious degrees of high fire potential" because they had high fire loading - excessively large quantities of combustible material for the buildings' capacities.

The James Watt Street and Kilbirnie Street tragedies were prime examples of fires taking place in buildings which had been converted from their original use: the James Watt Street factory had been a bonded warehouse with barred windows and the Kilbirnie Street cash and carry warehouse had originally been stables.

Chadwick castigated managements' short-sightedness - their "short cut method" and "take-a-chance attitude" - in failing to appreciate the value of fire prevention and fire defence.

The Firemaster had given the same stern message in previous years but he seemed to accept he was not getting far with "certain types of the business community and general public alike". The business types he referred to were small businesses that had sprung up after the war and had not seen the need to buy fire alarm systems.

Fire risks posed by individuals after the war included chimneys that had not been swept for years, portable paraffin heaters and even the parking of motorcycles and scooters in the kitchenette or under the stair. The Fire Service warned that "a leaking tank or carburettor can soon filll a room with vapour more dangerous than high explosives".

As people became more prosperous in the 1950s they wanted to replace their old kitchen ranges with smart ceramic fireplaces. Contractors often failed to replace the old hearth stone with something more heat and fire resistant. As a result timber joists underneath the fireplace could smoulder for days before igniting and causing dangerous fires, particularly in tenements where fire could spread quickly upwards through several floors.

Bill Wilson, who joined Glasgow Fire Service in 1957, remembers attending one particular hearth fire: "We went to a big, detached house in Hyndland where the people had been complaining for weeks about a smell of burning in an upstairs room where a new fireplace had been installed.

"When we got there we found a big fancy room where the fire had burned right along both sides behind the skirting boards. We finished up taking out a big section of the floor."

Firemen occasionally had to resuscitate people who had accidentally inhaled poisonous coal gas fumes from gas cookers or fires. Sometimes the gas would have been released as a result of carelessness in turning off taps. On other occasions the danger would have been caused by thieves cutting through gas pipes to steal slot meters containing coins.

Chimney fires were a common reason for bringing out the fire brigade. Firemaster Chadwick related one (possibly true) story about firefighters in the early 1950s attending a chimney fire in the home of an elderly lady.

Noting the filthy state of the chimney, the firemen asked when it had last been swept. The reply was soon after the last occasion the chimney had gone on fire. And when was that?

The old woman remembered the occasion very clearly because she had fed the horses while the firemen fought the outbreak. The lady was politely informed that Glasgow Fire Service had become fully mechanised before the First World War.

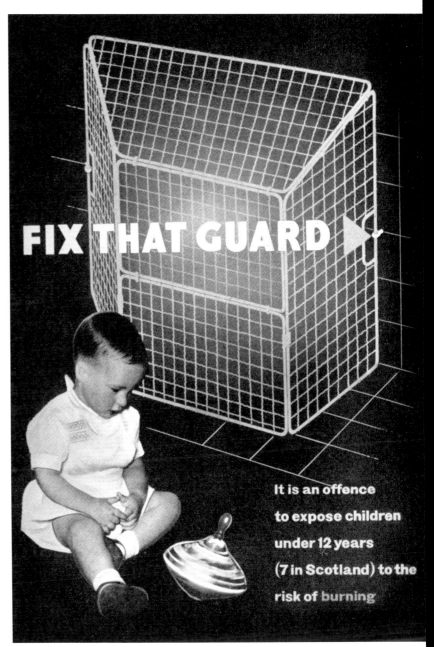

FIX THAT GUARD ▶

It is an offence to expose children under 12 years (7 in Scotland) to the risk of burning

Open fires were a big hazard in the home before central heating became commonplace.

EARLY DAYS

Glasgow has always had a strong bond with her firefighters, whether they were the firemen of the old Glasgow Fire Service and wartime National Fire Service or firefighters of both genders now serving with Strathclyde Fire & Rescue.

"Smoke Eaters" gather for the opening in 1900 of the Central Fire Station in Ingram Street.

Across the years, firefighters serving in the city have demonstrated courage, skill and resourcefulness, and the fire services have maintained a well-earned reputation for efficiency and innovation.

Glasgow was not always well prepared for emergencies, however. Early communities, including Glasgow, had houses that were usually built of wood and roofed with straw thatch. The houses tended to be packed close together along narrow streets and cramped closes.

An unorthodox way to test one of Glasgow's famous street alarms.

Naked flames were the only source of heat and light, so when accidents happened the effect could be disastrous. Glasgow suffered repeatedly from serious fires but the worst catastrophe occurred in 1652 when a fire broke out on the east side of the High Street. Fanned by a strong wind, the blaze spread south to the Saltmarket and then moved east and west along Gallowgate and Trongate. Within 18 hours, a third of the city had been destroyed and a thousand families made homeless.

At the time of this great fire of Glasgow, the city's firefighting resources were restricted to 24 water buckets and long cleiks or hooks for pulling burning thatch off roofs. By contrast, Edinburgh had its own early form of fire engine.

Risking loss of face on top of disastrous loss of property, the town council paid a

Early horse-drawn fire engine using steam power to pump water.

James Colquhoune £25 to build an engine identical to Edinburgh's for the "slockening of fyre". In May 1657, Glasgow took delivery of its first fire engine. The city's master of works was ordered to build a shed to house the machine beside Colquhoune's house at Candleriggs, prompting the thought that this structure was Glasgow's first fire station, and Colquhoune the city's first Firemaster.

Also in response to the 1652 fire, the council charged new burgesses "bucket money" to replace missing leather buckets. In 1654 the council paid for ladders which would be kept at strategic points around the city; two years later property owners were forced to keep ladders on their premises or face fines of "twentie pundis".

A fire in 1677, deliberately started by a disgruntled blacksmith's apprentice, destroyed 130 houses. This prompted the council to order new houses to be built of stone. This transformed Glasgow into a handsome city much admired by visitors such as Daniel Defoe.

The pumps on early fire engines were worked by levers. The water was mostly carried in buckets but the early 18th Century saw the introduction of the suction hose for drawing up water from local supplies.

A landmark year for firefighting was 1725 when the town council accepted an offer from the owners of sugar houses, or refineries, to volunteer their employees for fire duty. In exchange, the employees ceased acting as town guards.

An even more important landmark was reached in 1744 when a smith called Robert Craig was appointed Glasgow's first full-time firefighter. By 1747, Craig was in charge of 24 part-time firemen, each with his own strong leather cap, and three fire engines.

The 19th Century saw firefighting developments gather pace. The Glasgow Police Act of 1807 made fire extinguishing a role of the police who took charge of six manual pumping engines and 1,000ft of sewn leather hose.

In 1812 the Police Board decided that "two drums be got and kept in the Office to be beat in cases of fire and also that the Laigh Church (Cathedral's lower church) bell be rung." Later in the century, Glasgow's fire service took two major leaps forward in communications.

In 1861 every fire station became linked by telegraph to police and fire brigade headquarters and in 1878 Glasgow became the first UK city to install a street fire alarm system. Eighty-two alarm boxes were placed at the corners of the city's principal streets. In the event of a fire, a glass disc was broken and a knob was pushed to ring a bell at the nearest fire station. This would turn out the fire brigade to that particular location. In 1892 portable telephones were carried on the fire engines enabling the officers to plug into the street alarm and talk back to Brigade Headquarters.

Shortly before this innovation, Glasgow's first steam fire engine was purchased in 1870 for £500. The new engine could do the work of five old manual engines, pumping out 400 gallons of water a minute.

Most of that water now came from Loch Katrine, thanks to an outstanding feat of Victorian engineering completed in 1859. The introduction of this plentiful supply - vital for a city with a booming population and industry - made it possible for 1,000 hydrants to be installed round the city. This number rose to 4,000 in 1892 when the fire service became a separate body from the police.

In 1873, Glasgow became the third major port, after London and Liverpool, to establish a salvage corps, funded by insurance companies. The Corps, whose members were tasked with protecting property from the effects of fires in buildings such as factories and warehouses, was wound up in 1984 and its function taken over by Strathclyde Fire Brigade. The Corps' last headquarters was in Albion Street, next door to the old Scottish Daily Express building and a short distance from the Central Fire Station in Ingram Street.

In 1898 four firemen were killed when a wholesale chemists in Renfield Street blew up.

Drummer to summon Glasgow firemen on duty.

The 20th Century ushered in a major innovation with the purchase in 1905 of Glasgow Fire Service's first motor-vehicle - a 24 horsepower Wolseley first-aid carriage that was to spell the demise of the four-legged horsepower that the service had relied on to get its appliances to fires. At the start of the century, Glasgow Fire Service had 42 horses but in 1913 the last two horses, Kelvin and Tweed, were pensioned off and the brigade became totally motorised.

In 1906 the brigade took delivery of its first fire engine, a Mercedes with a Panhard engine, manned by ten men and capable of 30mph. Soon after, the brigade purchased its first turntable ladder, extending to 85ft.

Wallace the Fire Dog died in 1902. Wallace is said to have attached itself to one of the fire engines taking part in a procession. He ended up living in the Central Fire Station and running ahead of fire engines to fires. Visitors to Strathclyde Fire & Rescue's Cowcaddens complex are greeted by the stuffed remains of Wallace, displayed in a glass case.

One of Glasgow's worst fire tragedies occurred in 1905 when 39 people were killed and 24 injured in a blaze in a lodging house in Watson Street.

In 1914 the brigade found 68 per cent of its men going off to war. The Firemaster, William Waddell, wrote to Lord

Kitchener, the war secretary, and persuaded him to grant exemption from enlistment for recruits to the brigade.

In the 1920s two firemen were killed at a store fire and four others died under a fall of masonry. On a more positive note, the inter-war years saw the brigade buy its first closed-circuit breathing apparatus sets.

Training courses on the sets were arranged with the Mine Rescue Station in Coatbridge. By the 1930s firemen were becoming more familiar with this potential life saver and in 1938 a special rescue tender was fitted out and equipped with eight sets.

The Second World War brought several attacks on Glasgow by German bombers. The first serious attack was in September 1940 when a stick of bombs straddled George Square without doing major damage.

The most serious attack occurred when a bomb shattered the deck of the cruiser HMS Sussex and exploded deep inside her hull. Fuel oil went on fire, threatening the ammunition magazine, and it took Firemaster Martin Chadwick and his fire crews 12 hours to extinguish the fierce blaze. The ship was recommissioned and used for the surrender of the Japanese at Singapore in 1945.

In 1941 all of the brigades in Britain were brought under the umbrella of the National Fire Service and divided into zones. Glasgow and much of the west of Scotland stretching to Stirling became Western Zone 1. Glasgow's Firemaster, Martin Chadwick, became the Fire Force Commander of Western Zone 1 and had to organise firefighting cover to deal with the effects of enemy bombing.

By far the worst Luftwaffe attacks on Western Zone 1 were over the two nights of the Clydebank Blitz in March 1941. The bombing killed over 500 people and left the town devastated.

In 1941, Glasgow firefighters travelled on the Stranraer to Larne ferry to assist in Belfast after the city was heavily bombed. The officer in charge from Glasgow had overall command.

Later in the war, firefighters from Glasgow and other parts of Scotland were seconded to an American unit, General Omar Bradley's 12th Army Group, during the invasion of Germany in January 1945. The firefighters served for the duration fighting fire and protecting supplies needed for the advancement into Germany.

There were 27 firemen killed during hostilities in Western Zone 1.

MAJOR FIRES THROUGH THE YEARS

4 May 1949
Graftons fashion store, 43 Argyle Street

In the roll-call of disastrous fires in postwar Glasgow, one tends to be overlooked.

Glaswegians at least of a certain age will be familiar with the names of Cheapside, James Watt and Kilbirnie streets. On the other hand the Graftons fashion store fire of 1949 will probably fail to raise any flicker of recognition.

This is extraordinary, because the fire that claimed the lives of 13 young women - six of them teenagers - was witnessed by hundreds of people in Argyle Street, one of Britain's busiest thoroughfares; one of those victims died after she and a colleague jumped into the street to escape the fire. The crowd also watched as two male managers, who would later receive the George Medal, led five shopgirls out of a top, fourth-floor, window and along a narrow ledge to safety.

It was at 3 o'clock in the afternoon of Wednesday 4 May 1949 that two fire calls were simultaneously received at the headquarters of Glasgow Fire Service at the Central Fire Station in Ingram Street. One of the calls was made via a street fire alarm at the junction of Miller Street and Argyle Street, less than a mile from the Central Fire Station. The second call was made through the 999 telephone emergency call system.

The Central Fire Station responded by sending two motor pumps and a turntable ladder to the scene. At 3:03pm the officer in charge of the detachment sent back a message indicating that the fire was serious and people were trapped. The officer requested the attendance of ambulances and tramway overhead wiremen to cut off power to cables which were interfering with firefighting operations.

Receiving the message, Firemaster Martin Chadwick and his assistant, John Swanson, jumped into a car and headed to the scene.

In his report after the incident, Firemaster Chadwick wrote: "I arrived on the fire ground at 3:06pm but on the way to it I noticed dense volumes of smoke over the tops of buildings at

Crowds almost fill Argyle Street as a woman is led down a ladder to safety.

the junction of Ingram Street and Glassford Street. I remarked to Mr Swanson that the fire appeared to be very serious and was evidently 'well away'.

"On reaching Argyle Street I found that the traffic was completely jammed and it was almost impossible to make much progress without driving partially on the pavement on the wrong side of the road, which I did until I reached Argyle Street at the Glassford Street junction and then found difficulty in making further progress owing to the dense smoke which was completely obliterating visibility."

Chadwick stated that it was impossible to see whether the fire was on the north or south sides of Argyle Street. Hundreds of people, affected by the blinding smoke, were trying to get away from the area.

Chadwick and Swanson left the car and continued on foot to the burning building - the Graftons fashionwear department store at 43 Argyle Street, directly opposite Marks & Spencer.

"With difficulty," continued Chadwick, "we reached the front of the building and in a momentary, temporary clearance of smoke I noticed a woman lying bleeding on the roadway outside the shop from which dense volumes of smoke and fumes were issuing."

The first fire crews were trying to force an entry through the front of the shop, reinforced by three powerful jets of water. However Chadwick saw that the fumes were almost choking his men who were "displaying great courage and perseverance under extremely punishing conditions".

Firemaster Chadwick then sent his deputy, Swanson, to the rear of the premises to see if entry could be forced there. At that point he noticed four or five women on the roof of the adjacent Argyle Cinema. While firemen erected a ladder to rescue the women, Chadwick gave instructions to pitch two turntable ladders at the front of the building to pour water onto the blaze.

He also decided to supervise the work personally because of the risk involved in raising ladders beside live tramway cables that were invisible in the thick smoke. If cables were brought down into the congested street they would pose a danger not only to firemen but to the hundreds of people thronging the street or sitting in densely packed tramcars.

The Firemaster asked the first woman down the ladder if there were any other people in the Graftons building. "Although the woman was in a very distressed state she was able to tell me there was about 30 people."

Chadwick entered the cinema and went up onto the roof from where he could see that flames at the rear of Graftons "were reaching a considerable height and issuing with great ferocity." Firemen on the roof had to use their hoses to stop the fire spreading into the cinema.

At 3.18, with smoke starting to clear and police able to move traffic on, Chadwick called for ten extra pumps and more turntable ladders. He then ordered six men into breathing apparatus so that they could start searching the store. The main stairway had been destroyed, however, and barred windows hampered entry from the rear where firefighters were being showered with flaming debris as they poured water on the blaze. Heat from that blaze had bent the bars on the windows.

Finally, at 4pm, firemen gained access to the top floor where they found 11 bodies "lying more or less in a group between desks".

Firemaster Chadwick joined the firemen at the tragic scene: "I was satisfied that they were all dead as it was quite impossible for people to live in this building from the time of my arrival on the fire ground. In fact I formed the opinion from my observations of the positions of the bodies and the fact that their faces bore no traces of distortion that they had died of asphyxiation, probably carbon monoxide poisoning, within five minutes of the outbreak of the fire.

"I think they must have died very early and without pain."

The body of another girl was found on the second floor, beside a front window.

Deciding to inspect the charred interior of Graftons, Chadwick noted "with great concern" that doors leading to an emergency outside staircase were fitted not only with slipbolts but also lock bolts, and in at least one case the bolt was even padlocked.

The Firemaster doubted, however, whether the trapped persons would have been able to use the stairway as he was satisfied that the fire originated in the ground floor of the premises "and shot up the exposed lift shaft with terrific speed, entering all floors as it passed to the top of the building at a point which would have been en route to the emergency stairway via these doors at the rear of the premises."

The Firemaster's report continues: "The speed and rate of travel of the fire must have been abnormal. In fact, in the whole of my 27 years' service I have never seen a fire of this nature develop with such tremendous speed and to have simultaneously entered and covered every floor of the building.

"The wooden staircase leading down to the lower floors of the building would have been inaccessible owing to the travel of fire on these lower floors to anyone who might have been trapped on the top or second top floor. This more or less forced people to the front of the building and to attempt to escape via the open window and along a ledge onto the roof of the cinema."

Chadwick was referring to the remarkable escape masterminded by Solomon Winetrobe, a 29-year-old ex paratrooper who was in charge of the stock, and his assistant, George Platt. It was Platt who noticed that a sloping, five-inch wide ledge stretched to the roof of the cinema.

Escape route for Platt, Winetrobe and five shop assistants.

Fireman, still in wartime steel helmet, hacks through floorboards in gutted store.

Platt stepped out onto the ledge, grabbed hold of a rone pipe part of the way along and worked his way to the cinema roof. Winetrobe then followed on as far as the rone pipe which he held on to while supporting each of the five girls in turn as they were passed safely to Platt on the roof.

At the fatal accident inquiry held only seven weeks after the fire, John Cameron, the King's Counsel representing Graftons, controversially attempted to contrast the bravery of Winetrobe and Platt with the performance of the firemen.

Cameron had evidently decided that the best way to defend Graftons from allegations of negligence over fire safety was to attack Glasgow Fire Service. He persistently questioned Firemaster Chadwick and other fire officers as to why they had not pitched their ladders against the front of the store. The officers said that doing so in the face of a fierce blaze, blinding smoke and close to high voltage tramway cables would only add to the casualties.

Eddie Boyle, who joined Glasgow Fire Service in 1946 and was a fireman at the Graftons blaze, remembers the inquiry: "The fire brigade got torn to pieces. Chadwick had no counsel at all and he got torn to pieces."

Allan Reid, who served with the Glasgow Salvage Corps, remembered the officer in charge of the first fire engine at the scene being challenged by Cameron: "People trapped and it's too dangerous to attempt a rescue?"

Reid added: "The officer didn't get a chance to say the reason they couldn't put a ladder up was that the first fireman on that ladder would be dead."

Glasgow Fire Service members were convinced that the victims of the fire were probably dead by the time the fire engines arrived and that there had been a severe delay in calling the fire brigade, two minutes away in Ingram Street, because staff had spent time trying to extinguish the fire when it broke out in a ground floor compartment or "cubby hole" under the staircase.

Harry Palmer, who joined Glasgow Fire Service in 1948, said: "The first fire crew had smoke meeting them before they turned into Argyle Street. I always suspected that people, if they saw flames, didn't want to be the first to look for a telephone in case they missed some excitement."

In his summing up at the end of the inquiry, Cameron told the jury that Platt and Winetrobe had exposed themselves to "risk of death and injury in a manner which the Fire Brigade did not".

He continued: "It seems to me, having regard to the extraordinary character of the outbreak, that this was not a case in which the finger of blame could be pointed at the management. There was, to put it no higher, some lack of that dash and undaunted devotion to duty one is wont to associate with our fire services.

"Had the same determination, courage and skill been displayed by the public organisation as was displayed in a grave emergency by men like Winetrobe and Platt, you and I would not have been brought face to face today."

Cameron's hostile tactic did not pay off. The jury found that Glasgow Fire Service had functioned with efficiency. Furthermore, it found that the fixture of a padlock on the inside of the escape door on the fourth floor delayed exit to the fire escape and that owing to the inflammable nature of the stock and the extreme youth of many of the employees, Graftons should have taken specific precautions, for example fire extinguishers and an adequate warning system, against an outbreak of fire.

The lesson learned by the Fire Brigade was that it would have to have legal representation for any future inquiry to robustly defend their actions, which they themselves had to do at the Graftons FAI when confonted with an aggressive advocate representing clients who were very much the cause of that particular disaster.

Lines of hose trained on blazing Arnott Simpson's store.

3 February 1951
Arnott Simpson's department store, junction of Argyle Street and Jamaica Street

This was a massive blaze that destroyed a famous Glasgow department store, Arnott Simpson's, the Queen Anne Pub and a restaurant, and also threatened to destroy every block between Argyle Street and Howard Street. It took the courage and determination of 300 firemen operating from 15 fire engines, six turntable ladders and a fire boat to finally bring the fire under control.

The fire in Arnott Simpson's was already an inferno when the fire service was called. Luckily, the firemen had not had a chance to get out of their machines before the store's windows blew out and fire belched from every opening.

With the wind blowing from the west, the fire threatened the Adelphi Hotel, at the corner of Argyle Street and Union Street. Burning fragments and sparks were showered onto these buildings but fortunately a heavy blanket of snow on the rooftops cooled the embers.

The turntable ladders were positioned at key points round the fire to prevent its spread and allow firemen to tackle the blaze at close quarters. This stage of the battle posed particular risks for "branchmen" who had to avoid falling masonry as they directed their hoses at the fire.

There were some narrow escapes as parts of the building fell into the street and six firemen only managed to reach safety when the Queen Anne pub collapsed, sending tons of debris hurtling down.

Harry Palmer and his Central Station colleagues were in one of the first appliances at the scene: "We drew up at Arnott Simpson's and the shop windows blew out. So we whirled

Above: Firemen get in close to fire.

around and went to Boots Corner where we found a suction valve which enabled us to provide plenty water for the fire engines. We connected into the fire engine and provided many lines of hose to fight the fire."

Palmer remembers being served a cup of tea by the Salvation Army in the doorway of the Adelphi Hotel before he ended up at the top of a turntable ladder near the St Enoch tearooms (at the western end of what is now the Argyle Street pedestrian precinct).

Before work began to demolish Arnott Simpson's, added Palmer, earth had to be put down to cushion the fall of masonry because the low level rail line ran underneath the property.

16 March 1953
Leon & Co, Ballater Street

Four years after Graftons, Glasgow was shocked yet again by a fierce and deadly workplace fire, in the Gorbals premises of furniture manufacturers Leon & Co.

This day would turn out to be one of the proudest and the saddest in the history of firefighting in Glasgow.

At this incident members of Glasgow Fire Service earned three George Medals, two British Empire Medals and three Queen's Commendations for bravery, the largest number of civilian bravery awards ever awarded for a single incident. The tragedy is that the fire service members would not have been put into a position to earn their awards had two Leon's directors and three male employees not decided to extinguish the blaze on their own.

The fifth, top, floor of Leon's factory in 270 Ballater Street was used for furniture polishing and cellulose spraying. It is believed that a faulty fan in a spray booth ignited deposits of polish residue.

The fire spread so fast that staff could do nothing to control it so they fled to safety.

Catherine Anderson, forewoman of the cellulose spray section, told the Evening Times that after she heard a shout of "fire" she ran to the phone and told the twelve employees under her charge to get out.

"Being in charge I was the last to leave, of course, and I fell on the way downstairs choking with fumes. We all reached the ground floor and got out all right but I was so shaken that I don't know what happened after that," she added.

With the alarm raised on the factory intercom, the five men on another floor decided to take matters into their own hands.

Without realising that the staff on the top floor had safely escaped, the five decided to assist. The men seized fire extinguishers and took the lift to the top floor but when the solid folding door of the lift cage opened they were immediately hit by the heat and flame of what was now an inferno which had swept through the entire floor.

Four of the men died in or beside the lift, but a fifth, company director Thomas McLeish, was dramatically rescued by three senior fire officers including Assistant Firemaster John Swanson.

The firemen, alerted by cries for help, had forced their way to the top floor. Protected by covering jets of water, the three officers then fought their way through the flames to the lift and found McLeish was the only person still alive.

The fire officers carried the director back through flames to safety but he died two days later in hospital. While the rescue was taking place, firemen perched on turntable ladders overlooking the building directed water onto the seat of the fire

The George Medal was awarded to Assistant Firemaster Swanson, Divisional Officer James Melvin and Column Officer William Anderson; the British Empire Medal was awarded to Firemen John Blackwood and John Harrold; and the Queen's Commendation to Leading Fireman Martin McArthur and Firemen John Balmain and Alexander Morton. The eight men were also awarded the City of Glasgow Medal for Bravery.

In his annual report for 1953, Firemaster Martin Chadwick praised the courage and gallantry of the five Leon men: McLeish, Daniel Coorsh, Alfred Schmidt, William McGowan and James Gibb. He added: "The Glasgow Fire Service salutes the memory of these brave civilians."

Chadwick also wrote that his own men's gallantry had been "in the highest traditions of the Service". He pointed out how the life of Divisional Officer Melvin had previously "been despaired of" after he had fallen 90ft from a broken turntable. Melvin lay in a plaster cast for several months but recovered from his severe injuries to lead his men in many difficult situations including the Leon fire.

Meanwhile, 1953 featured another horrific case of a fatal fire in the workplace. A Glasgow firm which allowed an employee to carry two open pails containing the flammable oil naphtha was fined £10 for contravening a condition of its petroleum spirit licence.

The employee aged 16 lost his life when the naphtha caught fire while he was in a lift. The company had for 15 years allowed naphtha to be carried in open pails. The Stipendiary Magistrate rejected its argument that the licence simply referred to prevention of leaks or its vapour from its storage place.

The Glasgow Fire Service Officer who recovered the body said that the fire could have been caused by a spark or the employee smoking. The vapour was three times heavier than air and if it left a trail, a spark would cause a fire to flash back to the pails.

20 May 1953
Lyric Theatre, Sauchiehall Street

This popular theatre puts on its most dramatic show, unfortunately one in which fire is the main player. The blaze seriously damaged the main auditorium and destroyed the roof of the theatre which was a venue for Glasgow amateur theatrical companies. The Lyric was rebuilt but demolished in 1962 to make way for an office block.

Fires were a constant threat in Glasgow's densely packed theatres. The only major loss of life, however, occurred in 1849 in the Theatre Royal, Dunlop Street when a small gas leak ignited but was

Auditorium a scene of devastation.

safely extinguished. Someone shouted "fire" and in the ensuing panic, 65 members of the audience, mostly young people, were crushed to death on the stairs.

Fourteen years later, the Theatre Royal was almost totally destroyed by fire.

A former senior officer of Strathclyde Fire Brigade, Keith Small, remembers doing "theatre duty" as a young fireman in the Citizens Theatre some 30 years ago.

"You would go hours before the performance started and check that the theatre and fire escape doors were all right. Then you would stand on the prompt side of the stage just in case anything happened and then stay for an hour after the performance finished and the audience left," said Small.

15 October 1954
Thomas Graham & Sons warehouse, 17/21 York Street

If Glasgow was a tinderbox, warehouses provided much of the tinder. Huge 19th Century buildings, constructed with wooden floors and loaded high with flammable goods, they lined the narrow streets running north and south from the Clyde. A nightmare for a fire service requiring safe elbowroom to tackle big fires.

A police constable was on night foot patrol in York Street at around 21:20hrs when he saw signs of fire in a warehouse. He made a 999 call which was received at the Fire Service Headquarters' main control centre. Two fire engines, a turntable ladder and the fire boat were despatched to the incident.

The warehouse was actually two buildings situated east and west of a narrow courtyard on the west side of York Street. Fire crews discovered that the fire was in the west building so several jets were put to work.

With the fire growing rapidly, a message "Make pumps 8" was sent back and minutes later the west building collapsed, considerably increasing the intensity of the fire. The blaze now threatened the east building and a message was sent back at 22:05 to "Make Pumps 12 and Turntable Ladders 4".

Fire crews managed to save the east building despite the fact that the congested site made their line of attack on the fire limited, that fire doors had been left open and the fire load in terms of type and quantities of stored material greatly exceeded the recommended safety margin. To add to the potential risk, the building was next door to a tobacco warehouse, a whisky bond and a wine and spirit store.

17 January 1957
LEP TRANSPORT, 18 Houldsworth Street

Another big warehouse fire, and the Firemaster's annual report almost shouts with frustration that the building is not fitted with automatic detectors.

Over 100 people had to be evacuated from their homes in Argyle Street in Finnieston after a fierce fire broke out in the transit warehouse containing "an excessively wide range of goods and commodities".

The lack of smoke detectors meant that the fire was already a raging inferno, engulfing the roof and two topmost floors, by the time the first appliances arrived. Within a few minutes the roof and upper floors collapsed.

LEP is left an empty shell.

As firemen fought strenuously to control the fire and prevent its spread they were in constant danger of being hit by falling masonry from the 150ft long five-storey building.

Window panes in the evacuated flats in Argyle Street were cracked by the heat from the blaze, fuelled by the warehouse's contents that included bales of clothing, paper and furniture.

Firemaster Chadwick's report added: "There is no doubt whatsoever that automatic detection, with direct connection to the district Fire Station, would have prevented the serious consequences of devastation in this instance, but these observations, whilst appreciated and understood within the orbits of our own professional circle, are of little value unless they are widely circulated to reach the ears of those whom we would wish to advise in the protection and safe keeping of their business interests."

And as if foreseeing the time when cheap domestic smoke alarms could be bought off the shelf, the Firemaster continued: "It seems inevitable that the day is not too far distant when all classes of buildings and occupancies must universally be equipped with Automatic Detectors as an accepted part of the structural fittings or services and indeed the future must hope that some medium of automation will extend even to domestic premises. The modern development of multi-storey residential flats provide pre-installation of telephone, radio and television services etc. Why not Automatic Fire Detection?"

19 August 1958
Barrowland Ballroom, 244 Gallowgate

A Glasgow institution is reduced to cinders and twisted metal. And who's to blame? The fire investigation concludes that the most likely cause is a cigarette or still-burning match dropped carelessly by a person with a lot to lose from the fire - a musician.

Duty watchman James Clark was doing his rounds at around 06:14hrs when he heard the sound of crackling coming from the upper floor. He climbed the main stairway and entered the ballroom. At the far end, he saw flames near the door leading into the bar.

Joined almost immediately by a member of the maintenance staff, the pair tried to fight the fire on their own. When they realised they were not succeeding they retreated to the ground floor to phone for the fire service.

Fire crews had already arrived, however, alerted by people who had seen the fire from outside. As the fire grew in ferocity, about 40 people, some in their night clothes, hurriedly left their homes in an adjoining tenement.

Sam McIver, owner of the ballroom and the car saleroom beneath the dance hall, was one of the first on the scene. As the fire raged on the floor above, police and passers-by pushed about 40 cars out of the saleroom doors to safety.

The fire was finally extinguished after 12 water jets had been in use for about an hour. By that time the entire first floor had been destroyed.

The source area of the fire was traced to a confined space where band instruments and music were stored. Musicians had used this area to change into their ordinary clothes after the end of their performance around 23:00hrs the previous night. Fire investigators concluded that a likely cause of the fire was a match or cigarette hastily dropped by a band member in a hurry to get home.

Undaunted by the estimated £100,000 cost of the damage, McIver kept his promise to build a new Barrowland and the institution rocks to this day.

Opposite: Last night this was a ballroom...
but it would dance back to life.

28 January 1959
Fatal tram crash, Shettleston Road

The coincidence of a large lorry about to be reversed into an ironworks just as a tram appears on the scene led to the worst public transport accident in Glasgow for many years.

The No. 23 tram was crowded with passengers in the late morning as it made its way from Garrowhill along Shettleston Road to the city centre. Shortly before 10:00 the tram arrived at Parkhead Forge just as the driver of the big eight-wheeler was preparing to back into the entrance.

Instant inferno on the No. 23 tram.

The tram collided with the lorry, jamming it against a wall. The tram kept moving, ripping its nearside open against the end of the lorry and damaging its electrical switchgear. The main power cable carrying 600 volts was severed and a fire immediately broke out.

In seconds, flames leapt through the thinly-clad aluminium shell of the tram. Screaming passengers jumped from the top deck, many of them receiving broken limbs and severe burns.

The driver, the father of a year-old boy, and two women passengers were pinned into their seats by the impact of the crash which had driven the staircase back into the body of the tram. Firemen tried desperately to rescue the driver and passengers but the three died in the blaze. The Evening Times described how the fire was so fierce that drops of molten metal dripped down the sides of the tram and hardened as the flames were put out by fire hose.

At this time in Glasgow, the city's romantic affair with the tram car was nearing the end of the road thanks to rising fares, an ageing fleet and the growing challenge from bus services. In September 1962 services ended with a parade of old and new trams watched by a crowd of over 200,000 people.

1960

This was the year of the Cheapside Street Disaster, described at the end of this book. Even if the disaster had not taken place, 1960 would still have stood out as an eventful and challenging year for Glasgow Fire Service and Glasgow Salvage Corps.

It was the year when a fireman was killed and several colleagues seriously overcome by sulphur fumes from a cargo boat carrying burning matches. It was the year when Woolworth would have one of its city centre stores destroyed by fire and the other extensively damaged.

And it was a year when two transit warehouse fires within days of each other seemed to act as a warning of the Cheapside Street calamity to come. Both warehouses were extremely large and contained large quantities of goods. Fire damage to both was severe but fortunately both fires were prevented from entering adjoining warehouses by brick dividing walls fitted with fire-resisting doors.

Glasgow Fire Service's annual report for 1960 stressed, however, that both fires could have been stopped in their early stages if sprinkler systems and fire alarms had been installed in the warehouses.

Hoselines run from fire boat St Mungo to Cheapside Street.

28 February 1960
Prince's Dock

This two-storey warehouse measured almost a third of a mile long by 75ft deep. Its contents included 1,550 bales of jute bagging and 3,500 bags of groundnut cake. The fire, in the section containing jute bagging, was burning fiercely before it was detected just before 02:00 by a watchman. It took 107 firemen using 27 jets, including boarding with jets of water from a ship moored alongside, to extinguish the blaze.'

Surveying the wreckage at Princes Dock.

20 March 1960
Yorkhill Quay

Yet another case of the fire service being called too late. At 03:15 a watchman saw smoke coming from a stack of jute bales. He tried to tackle the fire with buckets of water while asking a colleague to summon the fire brigade.

Flustered and confused, the second watchman eventually hammered on the door of a neighbouring storage shed and told the watchman there about the fire. A call was finally made to Glasgow Fire Service, half an hour after the blaze was first detected.

The fire caused about £750,000-worth of damage, but fortunately it did not reach an adjoining warehouse containing a large number of Triumph sports cars awaiting export.

WOOLWORTH'S STORES FIRES

28 May 1960 -166 Sauchiehall Street

This was just the start of a nightmarish period for the popular store chain in Glasgow.

At 14:24 on this busy Saturday afternoon, Glasgow Fire Service received a 999 call to the Woolworth's store in Sauchiehall Street, one of the UK's leading shopping streets.

Staff and customers were evacuated and when the fire crews quickly arrived, they discovered that the entire stock area on the third floor was on fire. The crews had particular difficulty reaching the seat of the fire because of the smoke-logging and intense heat in the congested main stockroom.

Eight pumps and two turntable ladders were needed to bring the fire under control. Cost of the damage was around £43,000. The cause of the fire was suspected to be a dropped cigarette or match.

20 October 1960 - 36/48 Argyle Street

If Woolworth's were still smarting from the loss of trade resulting from the fire in their Sauchiehall Street branch, they were about to experience much worse at their other city centre store.

At 17:51 the assistant manager of the Argyle Street Store telephoned Glasgow Fire Service to report a fire in the premises. When fire crews arrived they found the store well alight.

Firemen entered the store and broke through the ground floor in several places in an attempt to tackle the seat of the fire in the basement. Just as it appeared that they were winning their battle a sudden fresh surge of fire swept up over their heads and broke through the glazed section of the roof.

Woolworth's 36/48 Argyle Street

At that moment, Allan Reid and colleagues from Glasgow Salvage Corps were outside the store. They were having a break from working in the smoke to cover up stock and enjoying a cup of tea supplied by the Salvation Army.

"Another salvageman had just put his cup to his mouth when we heard a 'swish'," said Reid.

He continued: "We turned round and we could see the smoke changing - brown, black, yellow - the indication of heat with the potential of a flashover. All of a sudden John Swanson (the Assistant Firemaster) and four or five men ran out.

"They just dropped the hose and ran and flames shot halfway across Argyle Street. That's the fastest conditions resulting in a flashover I've ever seen in my life; in the space of two minutes it was smoke to inferno."

Reid remembers hearing the sound of three sharp blasts on a whistle - a signal to the firemen to get out. Fourteen firemen received injuries while escaping from the building.

The fire service now had to reposition its fire engines and bring in turntable ladders to prevent the fire spreading to neighbouring properties. At the height of the blaze, 120 firemen tackled the blaze which had 27 jets directed at it.

The fire destroyed the store, removing a famous shopping landmark from the Glasgow scene. The loss was estimated at an enormous £380,000.

Evidence obtained from witnesses on the spot indicated that the fire started in the crowded basement store and had been burning for some time before it caused a flashover - where a growing fire suddenly becomes fully-developed and consumes anything flammable within reach.

The rows of timber shelves, only 2ft 6in apart, and the large quantity of flammable sales goods provided plenty fuel for a serious fire. Glasgow Fire Service concluded that the fire load in the basement was far in excess of good storage practice standards.

Opposite: Firemen battle blaze after surviving flashover.

2 December 1960
Prince's Dock, Govan

Eight months after the terrible death toll of Cheapside Street, Glasgow Fire Service loses another fireman in the course of duty.

The German cargo ship MV Pagensand was two days out from Gothenburg in Sweden when the captain reported that a fire had been detected in the hold containing a cargo of matches, wood pulp and paper. The captain decided he could make for Glasgow, telling reporters later that at that point his vessel was closer to Scotland than Sweden or Denmark.

The Pagensand - its hatches and air vents closed to seal the fire - eventually arrived in the Clyde on Thursday, 1 December and it tied up at Prince's Dock.

The following day, Glasgow Fire Service's fire boat, the St Mungo, arrived alongside and firemen led by Station Officer Douglas Mearns boarded the Pagensand. The hatches were removed to reveal smoke drifting up from the smouldering cargo.

Mearns and 10 firemen, all wearing breathing aparatus, went into the hold to tackle the fire but were immediately overcome by sulphur fumes from the burning matches.

The firemen were pulled back onto the deck where frantic efforts were made to revive them. Ambulances arrived to take the firemen to the Southern General where Mearns was found to be dead; the ten firemen, however, were able to leave after treatment.

Firemen help move cargo of matches while colleagues enter dangerous hold.

Firemen laid out on deck after inhaling sulphur fumes.

26 October 1962
St Andrew's Halls, Berkeley Street

Glasgow suffered a grievous loss to its cultural life as the result of this fire which totally gutted the halls, leaving only the facade and outstanding Granville Street entrance.

The suite of halls were opened in 1877 to provide a gathering place for the burgeoning population of the city's west end. The Grand Hall was famed for its acoustics, said to be the equal of any concert hall in Europe, and the renowned tenor Enrico Caruso stated during a visit to Glasgow that he had never found anything better.

An automatic fire alarm alerted Glasgow Fire Service at 05:02, and although units from the West Fire Station in Cranston were soon on the scene, the seat of the fire could not be quickly detected. When firemen tried to force their way into the building they were balked by dense smoke and then a severe build-up of heat.

The fire spread quickly through the building and the roof collapsed, leaving only a shell.

James Smith, who had arrived from the East Fire Station later in the morning for relief duty, was surprised at the devastation he saw.

Things could have been much worse, however: "The fire officers and crews did an amazing job in saving the facade of the St Andrew's Halls and also preventing the fire from spreading through to the adjoining Mitchell Library. If they had failed we would also have lost the biggest public reference library in Europe."

The area once occupied by the halls now forms an extension to the "Mitchell".

Although no cause for the fire could be found, it was suspected that a member of the audience watching an amateur boxing tournament had carelessly dropped a cigarette.

Opposite: Lord Provost (later, Dame) Jean Roberts talks with firemen who have helped to halt the spread of the fire from the street using turntable ladders and lines of hose.

17 July 1963
Pettigrew & Stephens department store, Sauchiehall Street

Less than three years after the Woolworth's blaze in Argyle Street, another major store is devastated by fire.

A member of the Pettigrew & Stephens staff died after being overcome by smoke but other employees as well as customers who were trapped in the store were led down ladders or lowered by lines to safety by firemen. The cost of the damage was estimated at £520,000.

Right: A young Hugh Fraser (right) visits the fire scene; three years later he became head of House of Fraser stores.

*Water jets pour into
Pettigrew & Stephens*

2 November 1964
Gordon Brothers Warehouse,
Glassford Street

Firemen heading to this incident from the Central Fire Station were warned to expect a hoax.

"The gaffers said the 999 call was suspicious because there was a lot of giggling on the line," said Hugh Welsh, "but when we turned into Ingram Street, Gordon Brothers was going like the clappers with smoke pouring out from top to bottom."

Welsh, a 20-year-old recruit at the time, was one of 100 firemen who fought the blaze which caused an estimated £500,000-worth of damage to the city centre furniture and clothing warehouse.

During the incident, two firemen got into difficulties in the burning building and one of them sounded an alarm. Another two firemen were ordered to don breathing apparatus and get the men out.

16 September 1966
Grandfare supermarket, Cowcaddens

Yet another store fire which tested the endurance of the firemen in attendance.

James Smith remembers fighting the blaze from a police station: "There was a narrow lane that divided Grandfare and the police station. I went into the police station where we had a line of hose pointed out of a window at the supermarket.

"A moment later the wall of Grandfare came down and filled up the lane. Our window was completely blocked and our line of hose destroyed. We thought we had been entombed but were able to escape through the offices."

Above: Blaze takes full hold of Grandfare despite massive efforts by Fire Service.

Left: Exhausted firemen take a break.

Martin Bonnar was a fireman based at Queen's Park Fire Station in Allison Street. He remembers arriving at the incident when the fire was in the basement of Grandfare, "and within half or three quarters of an hour it was up through the roof".

Salvagemen on the scene as Grandfare fire flares up.

15 November 1967
Cumberland Place

Station Officer William Clark of the South Fire Station collapses and dies while being involved in tackling a house fire that resulted in children's deaths.

14 January 1968
Hurricane Low Q

A night of 90mph-plus winds that would tear roofs apart, send chimney heads crashing through tenement flats and leave parked cars crushed under piles of rubble.

What would turn out to be the worst storm for 30 years began on the Sunday evening with a spell of high winds. After midnight the wind-speed increased, with gusts reaching 80-90mph around 03:00 and one gust hitting 102mph, breaking all previous records.

The situation was grave: 70,000 corporation houses had been damaged, 1,100 chimney heads had collapsed and 550 were in a dangerous condition, ready to topple over. Some 69 tenement buildings would have to demolished with another 131 seriously damaged.

Glasgow Fire Service immediately found itself on the front line, having to respond to more than 80 calls for assistance from people trapped in their homes. Between 02:00 and 09:00 fire service personnel rescued 73 people and attended incidents involving nine fatalities.

By mid-afternoon, urgent calls for help reached 200.

Firemen and members of Glasgow Salvage Corps would cover 283 damaged roofs with tarpaulins, remove 112 dangerous chimney stacks and remove rubble from 56 roofs by the time that, on 28 January, "Operation Storm Cover" was deemed to be successfully completed. Damage to property was estimated at £9 million.

Firemen Gardner and Murdoch remove rubble from a tenement in Dennistoun.

"This was a real disaster for the city," said James Smith, "A number of times the chimney heads would go through the tenement to the ground floor, taking everything with it.

"A family was killed in Clouston Street in Maryhill, and in John Knox Street the brigade was removing rubble from a man trapped in a bed recess when the weight of the rubble took them all through the floor into the flat below."

John Jamieson, a turntable ladder driver based at Partick Fire Station, slept soundly through the night of the storm and then got into his car to go to work as normal: "I drove along South Street towards the wee granary that was being built. A new wall had been put up but on this morning it was flat on the ground so I thought someone had crashed into it.

"I went into the fire station and I was told to get myself ready. I asked what for, to be told 'What do you mean what for? We've had a busy night - where have you been, another planet?'"

Jamieson used his turntable ladder to rescue people trapped in their tenement flats and to let householders back into their flats to collect valuables. One task close to his heart was coaxing a German shepherd dog to jump down from a landing after the stair had collapsed.

"I'm a German shepherd person," says Jamieson, who has one as a pet.

Like John Jamieson, fellow ex-fireman Hugh Welsh did not have his sleep disturbed by Hurricane Low Q: "When I looked out the next morning, I thought was there a war last night? I remember a fireman, John Reilly came out of a machine and was blown against a wall and broke both his wrists."

Tinderbox Heroes joint author James Smith, closest to camera,
and Paraig MacKay backed by Div Off. P McGill direct hose jet on blaze.

18 November 1968
James Watt Street Disaster

In terms of the number of lives lost, the fire at A J & S Stern's furniture factory eclipsed all the other dreadful fires that gave postwar Glasgow its Tinderbox City reputation.

But it is not only the number of people who died - 22 - that was so shocking. It was also the way they died, trapped in a blazing building, their escape blocked off by barred windows and locked fire escape doors. The factory was originally a whisky bond, hence the bars on the windows.

Glasgow Fire Service received the fire call to Sterns at 10:31. The first fire crews arrived four minutes later to find that the blaze was already so severe that a message "Make Pumps 10, persons reported" had to be radioed in immediately.

At the height of the blaze, 93 firemen were in attendance and turntable ladders and a new Snorkel water cannon poured thousands of gallons of water into the building. Despite the large turnout and the efforts of firemen wearing breathing apparatus the heat was so intense that rescues proved impossible.

Escape to the ground floor had been swiftly cut off when the hoist and main wooden staircase were rendered unusable by the blaze and the two fire escape doors, which were steel doors, on the first and second floors were afterwards found to have been padlocked from the inside.

There was no sign whatsoever of any of the casualties at the windows when the Fire Service arrived

Any hope for survival ended when the roof collapsed.

The dead were the director and an employee of a glassware company which occupied the basement and the top floor of the three-storey building, and 20 Stern's employees including the director, Julius Stern.

Bob Aitken, who was a Fire Prevention station officer at the Central Fire Station in 1968, remembers people in the crowd shouting to the firemen "Get the bars off, get the bars off." However the fire conditions and dense smoke emanating

Super heated smoke churns from Stern's factory.

from the factory windows were such that rescue attempts were futile.

The cause of the fire and its rapid spread was attributed to polyurethane foam used in making furniture.

Aitken said: "The polyurethane foam was stored in the big space underneath the open tread stair on the ground floor. People couldn't run downstairs because it was on fire and there was a steel door that took you to the escape stair but it was locked - don't ask me why."

Many attempts were made by the fire brigade to enter the areas where the workers were believed to be – exposing themselves to great personal risk. Attempts were made to enter the door which led from the factory and was the escape door onto the stairway in the adjoining tobacco warehouse.

Divisional Officer Peter McGill, Sub Officer Paraig MacKay and Fireman James Smith attempted entry through the fire door leading into the factory. They discovered that the door was constructed of heavy metal, providing, with the window bars, customs security for the previous occupiers of the building who had used it as a bonded warehouse.

The metal escape door could only be opened by the use of oxyacetylene cutting equipment. Assistant Firemaster Watt sent for the use of an oxyacetylene torch to cut a hole in the steel door.

When the Brigade finally got entry into the first floor they found approximately fifteen bodies at the windows and the remainder of the casualties throughout the factory.

David Russell was a fireman at the North Fire Station in St George's Road when he attended James Watt Street. He and a colleague climbed into the cage of a hydraulic platform and were raised to a high part of the burnt-out building where the last two bodies had been located. The pair wrapped the bodies in blankets and plastic sheeting and lifted them onto the platform and returned to the ground.

"The smoke had killed them and I believe it was the smoke that killed all the other ones as well," said Russell.

As to why the firemen did not cut the bars off, Russell said: "You naturally ask why couldn't you do this, why didn't you do that, could they (the firemen) put chains round the bars and pull? But they couldn't get near the windows, the fire was so intense."

The nine-day fatal accident inquiry into the James Watt Street Disaster ended with recommendations covering key issues such as bars on windows, the control of storage and use of foam plastics and power of entry into premises to cover all aspects of fire prevention. A small fine was imposed on the owners.

Clearing up after the tragedy.

3 November 1969
STV Studios, Theatre Royal, Hope Street

One member of Glasgow Fire Service dies and ten colleagues need hospital treatment before this very difficult fire is brought under control.

Fire crews were called at 16:12hrs to the Theatre Royal, which served at the time as the headquarters for Scottish Television. Smoke was seen issuing from the sub-basement, a warren of TV production rooms.

Teams of firemen searching for the seat of the fire had to work for a great deal of the time in total darkness in a smoke-filled atmosphere and exposed to intense heat.

A key feature of the firefighting operation at the STV Studios was the use of a relatively new special foam concentrate - Hi-Ex Foam. Large quantities of the foam were pumped into all the spaces in the sub-basement "warren" to smother the fire, which had threatened to destroy not only the Theatre Royal but surrounding buildings.

January 1971

A very serious fire took place on the Sunday morning necessitating rescues of bedridden patients, patients who were blind and had to be physically led to safety. The Fire Service was confronted with a very dramatic incident. Douglas Leitch as the initial officer in charge had many quick decisions to make which determined the satisfactory outcome of the fire. It was a very serious fire with a potentially disastrous outcome.

Leitch went on to become acknowledged by the British Fire & Police services as a leading authority in fire investigation. As a member of the the Institute of Fire Engineers he was asked to write a text book on Fire Investigation. This book is widely used both by the Fire investigating officer and by police involved in investigative work involving death by fire and fraudulant fire claims. He was awarded the MBE in 1989.

20 March 1971
Deanston Drive

Station Officer James Matheson collapses and dies while being involved in tackling a tenement flat fire.

1972

A grim year for Glasgow Fire Service as seven firemen die in the maze-like confines of a burning warehouse, and three months later a fireman loses his life while trying to save a woman trapped in a tenement fire.

25 August 1972
Kilbirnie Street Tragedy

This was a body blow to a service that still had not fully recovered from the Cheapside Street Disaster of 1960.

The fire took place on the premises of a cash and carry warehouse belonging to Sher Brothers at 70/72 Kilbirnie Street. The building, consisting of a ground floor and two upper floors, had originally been a stables but had been considerably modified over the years.

A 999 call was made to the fire service at 11:21 after an employee discovered smoke and flames on the top (attic) floor. This part of the building, which had been lined and partitioned with hard-board, contained large quantities of sales stock including clothing and drapery on shelving, some as high as 12ft, or in cardboard boxes.

Firefighters made a determined attempt to find the seat of the fire. Their task, however, was made extremely difficult because of the cramped and complicated layout of the attic floor and the density of the stock which allowed the fire to spread.

Twenty-five minutes after firefighting had commenced there was still no sign of the fire being brought under control. The officer in charge, Divisional Officer Andrew Quinn, ordered everyone out so that, it is believed, he could get silence to assess the blaze or to attack the fire from the outside through windows.

Fireman James Rook was obeying Quinn's order to leave the building when another fire officer spotted flames in the attic. The officer got Rook to help him turn a hose jet on the fire. Moments later, part of the stock collapsed on the two men, burying Rook and stunning the officer, who lay unconscious for some time before managing to quit the building.

Above: Model reveals confusing layout of attic where (scorched) clothing (top) was stored.

Left: Station Officer Dick Carroll shows concern as he logs breathing apparatus use. His uncle, Divisional Officer Andrew Quinn, was one of the dead.

When Rook was reported missing, an attempt was made to find him but two of the rescue party collapsed with exhaustion.

Divisional Officer Quinn, described later as "a man of outstanding courage and tenacity", was determined that Rook be saved. He led a second rescue party comprising Leading Fireman Alastair Crofts, and Firemen Iain Bermingham, Allan Finlay, William Hooper and Duncan McMillan back into the warehouse.

The rescue party, wearing breathing apparatus, got into the attic and found Rook. A fireman, Brian Murray, who was already in the loft, supported a shelving rack while Bermingham tried to pull Rook clear. When the rest of the rescue team took over from him, Murray dropped to his hands and knees and crawled through the dense smoke and tumbled down the stairs towards the first floor.

Murray, later praised by Firemaster George Cooper for his outstanding bravery in entering the building single-handed to save Rook, was dragged out of the warehouse just before flames shot across the ceiling of the first floor. The sudden flare-up engulfed the rescuers and Rook in a deadly upsurge of heat.

The flare-up was witnessed by Hugh Welsh, who was a leading fireman in charge of the South Fire Station's turntable ladder.

Welsh was on a staircase leading into the first floor where Salvage Corps members had earlier covered warehouse goods with heavy duty plastic salvage sheets. He was holding an empty hose, waiting for water to come through so that he could extinguish fire "trickling" over the first floor ceiling.

Welsh said: "The fire got bigger and bigger and the heat up there must have been terrific at ceiling level because the salvage sheets started to melt and then they started to catch fire - and it was whoomph!"

In his report after the fire, Firemaster Cooper stated that the salvage covers were only a secondary factor in the rapid fire spread. The "prime agent" was the hardboard ceiling completely covering the first floor ceiling.

It was Welsh and a fellow leading fireman, Jimmy Smith, who pulled Brian Murray out of the warehouse.

Welsh, who would receive the Glasgow Corporation Medal for Bravery, said about this episode: "You can read all the stories you like about firemen carrying people over their shoulders, well Brian Murray came down those stairs with his shoulders banging off every step, but he got out."

While the tragedy was unfolding inside the warehouse, reporters including Alex Wattie of the Evening Times were covering what appeared to be simply a dramatic fire.

Wattie said: "It was a very spectacular fire but we thought there was no-one in the building and no risk to life. We still thought there was no risk to life when the roof fell in."

Some 20 minutes after the collapse, however, a bystander pointed out to Wattie that the fire officer in charge of the BA (Breathing Apparatus) board, which indicated how much oxygen firemen would have left, was in a state of shock.

"It was then that I thought something very serious had happened and then very shortly after that a senior fire officer told us there were seven men inside and it was perfectly obvious they wouldn't have survived if they were under that collapse," added Wattie.

As at any other incident, control room operators had a key role to play in despatching appliances to the incident.

Liz McCreadie had only been working for three years in the main control room at Central Station when Kilbirnie Street took place: "It was make pumps, make pumps, make pumps. It was such a big fire that calls were coming in from places like Australia from relatives and these had to be handled by the switchboard.'

McCreadie, who retired from Strathclyde Fire & Rescue in 2009, added: "I remember a sub officer, who I think had been one of the first at the fire, coming into the control room later looking totally shocked."

Ann Welch, too, was a young fire controller, working in the South Fire Station which lost four firemen at Kilbirnie Street: Iain Bermingham, Allan Finlay, Duncan McMillan and James Rook.

Welch described how she was the day shift controller when a policeman telephoned the station to say the Sher Brothers cash and carry was on fire: "I immediately set off the fire bell, actuated the indicator panel in the appliance room - two pumps and a turntable ladder. Control called from Ingram Street and I informed them we were attending the call with Station Officer (Dick) Carroll in charge.

"The crews of the emergency foam tender and road rescue came down to the watch room and Jim Rook and Allan Finlay were chatting with me and hoping they would be involved in the call."

Soon after, Station Officer Carroll requested "Make pumps 5". Welch sent out the emergency foam tender, with Rook and Finlay on board. News quickly came through that there had been deaths, followed by confirmation of who had died.

"From that moment, the switchboard was alive with calls from the families of crewmembers including those who had died," said Welch.

The people of Glasgow were shocked by the second major fire service tragedy in 12 years. As had happened following Cheapside Street, a huge crowd lined the streets as hearses bore the bodies of the Kilbirnie Street victims to Glasgow Cathedral for the funeral service. The bodies of the seven firemen were then taken to the Necropolis where they were interred in the vault under the Cheapside Street memorial.

Left: Firemen bear the coffins of fallen comrades out of Glasgow Cathedral.

Right: Members of the public join in service relayed outside cathedral.

18 November 1972
Maryhill Road/Great Western Road

On this day, Glasgow Fire Service lost a gallant comrade and found itself fighting fire on two fronts.

Fire crews were initially called to a fire which had broken out in a disused shop on the ground floor of a tenement block in Maryhill Road, near the junction with Great Western Road at St George's Cross. As the firemen worked hard to save flats above the shop, the fire found a way through to a row of tenements in Great Western Road.

The route that the fire took was a single-storey structure connecting back shops in both Maryhill Road and Great Western Road. Because the structure occupied part of the back courts between the two rows of tenements much of it was out of the reach of water jets.

The fire service had to bring in extra appliances to tackle the blaze that was now taking hold in Great Western Road. Firemen rescued 15 people by ladders and over 200 people were led through smoke to safety or evacuated from adjacent premises.

Meanwhile Sub Officer Adrian McGill sacrificed his life trying to save 48-year-old Miss

Women hurrying from the fire scene.

Alice Mulgrew who was trapped in her top floor flat on Maryhill Road. McGill succumbed to the effects of smoke inhalation after he got Miss Mulgrew to use his breathing apparatus. Firefighters rescued Miss Mulgrew by ladder but she died soon after.

A dreadful aspect of this event was the fact that some residents in the Maryhill Road flats had smelled burning around ten hours before the first 999 call was made. This gave time for the fire to reach the scale that it not only claimed two lives but resulted in the destruction of 41 homes, six shops, two public houses and a post office.

James Smith, who fought the fire in Great Western Road from the top of a turntable ladder, said: "It later emerged in the fatal accident inquiry that the spread of the fire to Great Western Road was the result of a building defect of about 100 years before. The builders hadn't put in a fire wall in the building extension which linked the two streets."

THE CHEAPSIDE STREET DISASTER

On the evening of 28 March 1960 the worst disaster in the peacetime history of the British Fire Service took place. It would be an event that would stun a city, shock a nation and raise sympathy and concerns around the world.

It was a night that Glaswegians would remember with dread, sorrow and a sense of awe. It was the Cheapside Street Disaster.

Three Glasgow Fire Service stations and also Glasgow Salvage Corps would be directly swept up in the disaster through loss of life. All other fire stations within the city boundary and many from outside Glasgow would also become involved in dealing with the aftermath of a massive explosion and tackling the enormous blaze that would be fuelled by over a million gallons of alcohol.

Aerial view of devastation.

The day started quietly in one of the fire stations to suffer a fatality - the West Fire Station in Cranston Street. Firemen from this station attended only one incident before the catastrophe that would take place that evening.

According to the fire station's log book, now displayed in Strathclyde Fire & Rescue's offices at Cowcaddens, that first incident was a run-of-the-mill job, a chimney fire.

The area control centre had received a 999 call at 00:49hrs to the fire at 305 St Vincent Street. A fire engine was sent to the scene and, with the aid of a stirrup pump, the fire was extinguished within half an hour.

SEARCH FOR THE FIRE

The search was on to find the seat of the fire. Peter McGill, the Station Officer in charge of the Central Fire Station, entered Section 2 of the building from Cheapside Street. He met Sub Officer Calder who reported that he had ordered two men to don breathing apparatus to carry out a thorough search of the building.

McGill and Calder went up to the first floor and found thick smoke but no great amount of heat, just the sound of fire crackling. McGill returned to Cheapside Street, ordered the Central's turntable ladder to be advanced along the street to be ready for any fire showing from the upper floors. McGill then donned breathing apparatus and with Firemen Jack Muir and David Gladstone they re-entered the warehouse at Section 2 and searched from ground to roof level but found no signs of fire.

Jack Muir's set was a half hour duration salvus oxygen set and when the exit whistle blew McGill ordered them out. Jack Muir remembers searching the warehouse, that the fluorescent lights were on and there was a fine mist within the warehouse. The mist had a stinging effect on his skin as if aftershave had been applied - reflecting that it could have been alcohol vapourizing.

Turntable ladder engulfed in flames as alcohol fumes ignite in mid-air.

As this was taking place, a separate party, led by Divisional Officer James Watt, based at Central, was carrying out a similarly fruitless search of Section 3.

The situation was now very serious, as Firemaster Martin Chadwick would explain in his report following the disaster: "Conditions on the Cheapside Street frontage were causing considerable anxiety having regard to the nature of the occupancy, the smoke-logging and, in particular, the absence of any heat conditions, suggestive that they were not nearing the area or seat of the actual fire, this despite the fact that firemen had been able to penetrate to the topmost levels of Sections 2 and 3."

Once more out in Cheapside Street, Station Officer McGill was informed that in Warroch Street firemen had seen flames inside the warehouse's Section 1, the main building occupying the centre section of the premises. Moving round to Warroch Street, McGill found that firemen had set an extension ladder against a barred window on the ground floor and had fed a hose through the bars and wire mesh in an attempt to douse flames licking across the ceiling. The flames had a purple-blue colour associated with alcohol.

Around this time, Arbuckle, Smith's managing director, Ronald Johnston, had arrived at the scene, attracted by the clamour of fire engines heading towards the Anderston Quay area. Johnston offered to help Glasgow Fire Service gain access to Section 1. Under his guidance, firemen used heavy axes to break through an emergency door in Warroch Street.

The firemen discovered, however, that the door led into an adjoining tobacco warehouse. The firemen now switched their attention to the rear entrance to Section 1 where the fire

had been seen. This door, metal-lined and bolted internally, was putting up much stiffer resistance to blows from a fire axe.

At this point, at 19:48 hours, Assistant Firemaster John Swanson requested "Make pumps 8" and moments later the Cheapside Street Disaster took place.

A fireman on top of a turntable ladder looks tiny against the blaze in this photograph taken a considerable distance away.

however; Tommy Hammond, who had only joined Glasgow Fire Service in the previous year, was ordered by Charles Biggerstaff to fetch some piece of equipment seconds before the explosion took place.

Hammond's widow, May, explained: "So Tommy ran up the road, and as he did the building fell out behind him and just covered the wagon."

Hammond survived to enjoy almost 30 years in the fire service.

Fire crews in Cheapside Street were so involved in their own drama that they understandably did not realise that the wall at the rear of the warehouse had also blown out, onto Warroch Street. It was in Warroch Street that Glasgow Salvage Corps lost all of its five members killed in the disaster and Glasgow Fire Service lost eleven firemen.

Raymond Ferrari, aged 23 and a trainee fireman, was in Warroch Street, standing beside the firemen who had set the ladder against the ground floor window.

"They were senior firemen and they asked me to give them more line (of hose). I turned my back to pull more hose in for them when the walls blew out. I was blown under our turntable ladder, which protected me to a certain degree. When I got up I was covered white with dust and all I could see were burning whisky barrels."

Minutes earlier, Bob Scouller had driven the Salvage Corps' first tender into Cheapside Street, but then an officer told him to continue round to Warroch Street "because that's where the action seems to be."

Before setting off for Warroch Street, Scouller told the driver of the Corps' second tender, Jimmy Harvie, to park his tender on the opposite side of Cheapside street, away from the warehouse.

"I wasn't thinking there'd be an explosion, I just thought our tender would be in the way of the fire engines if it was close up to the building. Jimmy told me afterwards: 'Bob, you saved my life'."

Scouller, accompanied by colleague Joe Smith, took the tender into Warroch Street. Meanwhile the five other crew members walked back down Cheapside Street to Anderston Quay and then started to make their way up Warroch Street.

Scouller explained what he saw when he and Joe Smith arrived in Warroch Street: "There were hoses lying all over the place. They were full and there was a big turntable ladder and also a pump and both of them were pumping like the clappers, hammering away, so there must have been something serious someplace."

It was normal practice for the Salvage Corps to get close to burning buildings, if it was deemed safe, so that salvagemen would not have far to carry heavy-duty plastic covers used for protecting property from water damage. Scouller asked Smith to help him move lines of hose so that he could manoeuvre the tender. Both men believe that the few moments spent completing this task probably saved their lives because it delayed their meeting up again with their colleagues who had been walking up Warroch Street from Anderston Quay.

Joe Smith was moving a line of hose when the Salvage Corps crew approached him: "I needed a hand so I said to them, kidding them on, 'Where have you been?'. They were about 15 to 20 feet from me when the building exploded. When I came to I had debris all over me. I was on the ground but I didn't know much about that."

Moments before the explosion, Bob Scouller passed the firemen "hammering away" at the ground floor window through which flames had been seen.

He said: "So I said to myself 'I'm not happy about this at all' and decided to turn and go back to my vehicle in case I had to move it.

"On the road back I passed the firemen again and one of them shouted 'Driver.' I said I was Salvage Corps and he said 'No, you're a driver. We're looking for an axe.' I said our equipment wasn't very good, not as good as the fire brigade's so I said 'I'll tell the driver of your pump you want an axe.'

"The fireman said 'Okay' and I just turned my back and walked a few steps when all of a sudden there was a 'whoomph'. I turned round just in time to see the building burst open and all the big, huge masonry falling down."

Scouller believes he had been standing only about 15 feet from where the masonry hit the ground.

Hose weaves a spaghetti trail as firemen pour thousands of gallons of water on the inferno.

He added: "The firemen I had been talking to, they ran but if they had run up Warroch Street they might have escaped it but they ran from the side of the building out towards the middle of the road. The building just came down on top of them and they were gone."

The South Fire Station's turntable ladder that had provided some shelter for Raymond Ferrari after the explosion threatened to be a death-trap for William Watters, the fireman perched at the end of the ladder about 50ft above the street.

From his vantage point, Watters could see firemen trying to force their way through the metal-lined door and several salvagemen standing on the pavement on the opposite side of the street.

Suddenly, Watters heard a loud bang. In his report he wrote: "There was a sort of blast and debris was flying all around me. I felt the ladder swinging away from its position and the next thing I realised was that I was actually looking into a building on the opposite side of the street. I was hanging from the ladder, held only by my safety belt."

Leading Fireman Robert Clark, who was in charge of the TL, later described how he shouted to Watters to start coming down the ladder as flames and smoke were enveloping the appliance. James Dunlop, however, said that he could bring Watters to safety by lowering the ladder. This was no simple task as the front of the TL had been badly damaged by falling masonry and its engine had stopped.

Dunlop was able to restart the engine by pressing a button at the rear of the TL. To bring Watters down, he then had to extend the ladder to release if from its pawls or safety locks. Once the ladder was released it was lowered by gravity and Watters got safely back to the ground.

A daunting vantage point for this fireman at the top of a fully-extended turntable ladder.

While all this was happening, whisky barrels were rolling from their racks in the bond and smashing open, adding to the rivers of burning alcohol flowing down Warroch Street.

Robert Clark later praised James Dunlop "for the calm manner in which he carried on after the explosion". Dunlop's determination to stay put and make sure that Watters was brought down safely while the flames were advancing round the TL earned him the George Medal.

Dunlop described the scene as he was bringing Watters down: "The back of our machine at this stage was clear but the flames were spreading rapidly and the whisky barrels were going boom, boom, boom."

The exploding barrels did not distract him from the task in hand: "I was too intent. I had put him (Watters) up there so I felt it was my responsibility to get him down before I departed the scene."

Leading Salvageman Bob Scouller had seen the TL catch fire as the whisky barrels tumbled into the street: "It was as if there was a giant up on top of the building and he was lifting them and tossing them into the street. The barrels were piled high and rolling... as one burnt underneath the next one rolled down, bumped down, was hitting the top of the building and stotting right out into the middle of Warroch Street."

The scene added to the anguish that Scouller had already suffered as a result of seeing at least four firemen being buried under the rubble and fearing that his crewmates had suffered the same fate. Immediately after the explosion he had run round to Cheapside Street to seek help and find his chief officer, Thomas Mundell. He discovered that the situation in Cheapside Street was as bad as in Warroch Street and when he told Robert Mundell "I think our men have gone.", Mundell replied: "Oh God, don't tell me that."

Both men decided to look for the salvagemen, with Mundell walking down Cheapside Street to the river while Scouller would return to Warroch Street. Back in Warroch Street, Scouller decided to reverse his tender out of harm's way but could barely get the key into the ignition because his hand was shaking. Once he had reversed up, he stood on a wing of the tender to look over the top of the rubble for any sign of his colleagues but there was none.

"I went back to Cheapside Street and got hold of Mr Mundell and said "Mr Mundell, there's nothing there.""

Hanging on to hope, Mundell replied: "I've been round and I can't see anything, but maybe they've been lucky, maybe they've got into a building some place."

Both men waited for some sign of their colleagues and when a BBC television crew appeared and asked Scouller if they could interview him, he refused. "I said to myself I'm not going on, I'm not going to break down. I felt rotten, really, and I said to them 'Not now'."

With the fire now "developing with tremendous speed", Firemaster Martin Chadwick sent out a request at 20:12hrs to "Make pumps 15", followed eight minutes later by a request to "Make pumps 20".

THE BLAZE ERUPTS

Divisional Officer John Evans, who had left the scene briefly to take Charles Biggerstaff to hospital, returned to find "an awe-inspiring fire of gigantic proportions." The fierce glow from the flames lit the night sky over Glasgow and clouds of alcohol fumes drifted up through the air to ignite, like giant distress flares, hundreds of feet above the city.

The scene was described by Bob Aitken, the day shift station officer at Central Fire Station who had gone with his wife Ann to see a play at the King's Theatre. When they came out of the theatre they saw a glow in the sky and Aitken decided to show his wife what a fire looked like.

"I had never seen such flames. You got pockets of gas going up and igniting away up there. Big tongues of flame, a space, then more tongues of flame up on the top. It was remarkable - horrific, as a matter of fact," said Aitken.

Down on the Clyde, passengers boarding the Royal Scotsman bound for Ireland were hit by flying embers and an ore carrier had to be hastily moved to safety.

A roll call was taken to find out which members of Glasgow Fire Service and Glasgow Salvage Corps were missing. The tally revealed 14 firemen and 5 salvage corps missing presumed dead but it was decided that it would be too dangerous for any attempt to rescue survivors or recover bodies while the fire was still raging.

Next morning, high volume monitors deluge the ruins of the bond.

Page from the West Fire Station's log book records the dead.

The personnel who died were:

Glasgow Fire Service

Sub Officer James Calder, based at the West Fire Station; Sub Officer John McPherson and Firemen Christopher Boyle, Alexander Grassie, Edward McMillan, Ian McMillan and William Watson, all based at the South Fire Station; and Firemen John Allan, Gordon Chapman, William Crocket, Archibald Darroch, Daniel Davidson, Alfred Dickinson and George McIntyre, all based at the Central Fire Station.

Glasgow Salvage Corps

Deputy Chief Salvage Officer, Superintendent Edward Murray, Leading Salvageman James McLellan and Salvagemen Gordon McMillan, James Mungall and William Oliver.

The main priority for the fire service was to contain the fire and prevent it spreading to neighbouring premises which included a Distillers Company Ltd whisky bond directly opposite the blazing warehouse in Cheapside Street and a Harland & Wolff engineering works in Warroch Street.

Divisional Officer James Gray from the South Fire Station was put in charge of protecting the DCL bond. Eight lines of hose were brought into the bond and then directed through its windows into the heart of the fire in the Arbuckle, Smith warehouse.

Gray soon discovered that part of the roof of the DCL bond had caught fire so he smashed a skylight and climbed onto the roof with colleagues to investigate. Gray and his colleagues went along the roof and broke back into a different section of the bond where window

*Diminutive figures of
two firemen reveal scale
of the disaster.*

frames had caught fire. A line of hose which the firemen had hauled along with them on their rooftop expedition was used to extinguish the flames and cool down barrels, believed to contain whisky, which were steaming in the heat.

Meanwhile in Warroch Street, firemen had to break down the entrance into Harland & Wolff's as staff had been sent home for their own safety. The priority in this premises was to ensure fire did not threaten a large stockpile of metal cylinders containing liquid oxygen and air.

"There were hundreds, possibly thousands of cylinders there and we were terrified in case they overheated and exploded," said Bill Wilson who was a fireman based at Knightswood Fire Station.

Wilson and his crewmates were inside Harland & Wolff's making the cylinders safe as his father and younger brother arrived on the fire ground to find out if he was still alive.

Wilson added: "You got it quite often at fires that crowds would turn up and at Cheapside there were massive crowds because you could see the fire from all over the city. I spoke to one Divisional Officer who could see the glow in the sky from his home in Dunblane."

The fire caused severe congestion on Glasgow streets. Margaret Davidson (nee Welsh) was due to start back shift at 23:00hrs as a firewoman/telephonist in Glasgow Fire Service's main control room in the Central Fire Station. When she heard about the fire on the 9 o'clock television news she decided to go to work straight away.

Davidson said: "I was visiting a friend in Bridgeton. I tried to get a tram car but I think the traffic was probably held up because of the fire so I took a taxi. When we arrived at the fire station the driver would not take money for the fare - he knew there was a big fire and he said to me 'Oh no, you're going in to work'."

That was not the only time Davidson had reason to be grateful to a taxi driver: "Half of Glasgow would have burnt down in those days had it not been for taxi drivers telling us about smoke or fires they had seen late at night. There were fewer people about late at night then to see if there were fires."

Opposite: Grim faces reflect tragedy.

Davidson remembers "the radio going like mad" with messages coming in from the fire ground. A particularly poignant aspect of the back shift was the telephone calls from exiles in places such as Canada or Australia who were inquiring about the wellbeing of relatives in the fire service.

Back on the fire ground, the battle continued to control the blaze. Felix Lennon, a fireman based at Govan Fire Station, was in Warroch Street, directing a hose towards burning barrels. He remembers being soaked by hoses held by colleagues standing behind him.

"The guys were just flooding it and I was just drowned," said Lennon, "There was a big sheet of corrugated iron and I grabbed it and held it right over me - at least I was getting a bit dry.

"I don't know how long I was there keeping this fire at bay when I heard a knock, knock, knock. It was a sub officer, Eddie McLean, and he said 'Is this where you've been? I thought you were lost, we couldn't find you'."

After the dramatic incident involving the turntable ladder in Warroch Street, James Dunlop found himself up to his knees in water inside a factory while directing water from a hose at the fire.

"There wasn't anything glorious, the fire had to be put out as it was still raging," said Dunlop.

In fact around midnight - five hours after the 999 call - the fire still had the potential to pose a severe threat to life and property. The fire had reached No 4 section which had storage vats in the basement. One of the vats exploded, bringing down the entire west wall of that section.

Gradually, what Firemaster Chadwick described as the "most tenacious and resourceful response by all ranks" resulted in the fire being brought under control at 06:18 on the following day, 29 March. Another major factor in quelling the fire was the presence of the new fire boat St Mungo, launched on the Clyde only 10 months before the Cheapside disaster. The St Mungo, which cost £80,000, had the capacity to feed water from the Clyde through 31 lines of hose to fire engines surrounding the fire.

FIRE SERVICES IN MOURNING

The sheer scale of the disaster and the heavy media presence at Cheapside Street and Warroch Street ensured that the world at large knew very quickly that something terrible had happened in Glasgow. In fact television and radio stations and Glasgow cinemas issued a message from Glasgow Fire Service calling on off-duty firemen to report to their fire stations.

For Glasgow Fire Service and the Salvage Corps there was the distressing task of informing and comforting wives and families and bolstering morale among personnel who had lost colleagues. Eighteen of the victims were married and 13 of them were fathers.

Station Officer Bob Aitken was given the task of visiting the homes of about seven of the firemen who had been killed and confirming to their wives or other relatives that the men were dead.

"The Central Fire Station, it was like a pit disaster with all the women there asking 'What's happening, what's happening?' I was told by a Divisional Officer that I had a job to do and I was given a list of names and addresses of the people who had been killed and I had to knock on the door and tell their families."

Aitken began his task early in the morning, around 01:30: "It was very harrowing. The wives wanted to go down to Cheapside Street but I had to tell them that there was nothing to see because they hadn't got them (the bodies) out."

The 19 are laid to rest.

William Oliver was aged only nine when his father, Salvage Corps member William senior, was killed at Cheapside Street. He was in bed when his mother received the news: "I remember wakening up and hearing what I thought was hysterical laughter. My mother had a laugh that on more than one occasion stopped the show in the Glasgow Pavilion theatre. It was like a donkey braying, and there were times when the comedian, Larry Marshall or Lex McLean or whoever, would stop and say something like 'Madam, you are stealing my thunder'."

The next morning, Mrs Oliver came up to William junior's room, and he discovered that the sounds she had uttered had not been laughter.

On a night when courage and selflessness was to the fore, the opposite extreme of behaviour was demonstrated by a sneak thief who called on the mother of one of the youngest victims, 25-year-old Fireman Edward McMillan, to inform her that her son was dead.

Edward's sister, Kay Crosbie, said: "The crook chapped my mother's door about midnight and said 'It's about your son.' My mother's purse was on top of the sideboard and he lifted it but then threw it down and ran when she shouted to my dad.

"My mother died six years after Edward, she never got over his death."

The family of George McIntyre, one of the firemen killed in Cheapside Street, learnt of the tragedy when they were watching television in their home, a flat above the fire engine bay at the North West Fire Station in Kelbourne Street.

George McIntyre's son, Tommy, who would go on to to be a fireman himself, said: "We were watching the western series 'Wagon Train' when ITN cut through the end credits just before nine o'clock to announce 'A disastrous fire in Glasgow, four killed and 17 injured.' As soon as we heard this, the whole place lit up and women were running down to the watch room crying and asking 'Is there any news?'"

Tommy McIntyre was driven by a friend to Cheapside Street to ask about his father. Fire officers he encountered told him they had no news for him, but he is now convinced they could not face telling him that his father was dead.

Tommy McIntyre spent a few more minutes in Cheapside Street helping a lorry driver to offload petrol cans needed for the fire engines which were pumping thousands of gallons of water onto the fire. He then returned home and the family were formally told around 22:30 that George McIntyre was dead.

The following morning, Assistant Firemaster Swanson visited the McIntyres. "He was upset," said Tommy McIntyre," and he told my mother 'I've lost the best of my men'."

Also on that morning, George McIntyre's brother, Robert, was travelling into work on the bus when he read in the paper that George was one of dead. "He was absolutely distraught," said Tommy McIntyre.

Robert Scouller was on his own as he drove his tender back to the Salvage Corps headquarters. He knew there was no hope for his five colleagues and he dreaded meeting their wives who lived in flats on the premises.

"As I was driving back I could see the collar and tie which Eddie Murray had removed and hung up in the tender on the way to Cheapside Street. It was swinging about and that made me feel worse," he said.

When Scouller got back to the headquarters he opened the garage doors quietly. In the back court he heard women crying and shouting "Where's my man?"

"I couldn't go out and face them, I couldn't tell them."

Soon after, Chief Officer Mundell arrived and spoke with the women. Scouller, meanwhile, went upstairs to his own flat to join his wife Heddie and ten-year-old son Richard. Heddie then went next door to comfort one of the widows.

At the South Station, an experienced fireman, Colin Higgins, was deliberately drafted into the squad which had lost six men.

Raymond Ferrari, who had to be taken to hospital suffering from shock and severe bruising to his back which had absorbed the shock of the explosion, remembers Higgins: "He was already in the South Station, a hell of a nice guy. He was brought into our squad where morale was way down and he was a morale booster with a good sense of humour.

"I remember him saying 'Look son, there's not enough darkness in this world to put out a penny candle'."

Vi Aitken, who was in her 90s when sadly she died shortly after being interviewed for this book, was senior leading firewoman in charge of the watch which came on duty at the control room in the Central Fire Station on the morning of 29 March. She remembered that Mary Nicoll, in charge of the previous watch that had to deal with a barrage of calls from the start of the disaster, was deeply affected by the tragedy for some time as were members of her watch. Nicoll was awarded the British Empire Medal for her services.

Although the fire was under control on the Tuesday morning, fire and salvage crews had to remain on site for several days to ensure that the fire was completely extinguished, to protect property from further water damage, and, especially, to locate and remove bodies of fallen comrades.

The service at St Andrew's Cathedral was led by the Archbishop of Glasgow, Donald A Campbell, who said that the day was one of the saddest ever in the history of the great city of Glasgow.

The service in Glasgow Cathedral was relayed through loudspeakers to the crowds outside. The Minister of Glasgow, the Rev Dr Neville Davidson, said that the "brave men who so tragically died left something precious that would live." They had left a legacy of duty done and determination and courage in the face of danger, of self-sacrifice "that would add luster to the records of the city."

The interment at the Necropolis took place in a biting wind. Each of the coffins was carried by six fire servicemen. The family members of each victim paid their respects as the coffin was lowered into the ground.

When the service ended, the mourners stood as Pipe Major Thomas Renton of the Glasgow Fire Service Pipe Band played the Flowers of the Forest. Finally, Firemaster Martin Chadwick, fellow officers of Glasgow Fire Service and officers of Glasgow Salvage Corps approached the grave individually to salute their dead comrades.

There was a fitting postscript to the ceremony on the following year when a stately monument funded by Glasgow Corporation was unveiled by Lord Provost Jean Roberts to commemorate the disaster. The memorial is a gathering point each year for ceremonies to honour the fire service personnel who died at Cheapside Street and also at Kilbirnie Street, in 1972.

1961: Cheapside Memorial unveiled.

Opposite: Crowds stand silent as cortege makes its way up High Street to Glasgow Cathedral.

Other fire services expressing sympathy included those of Barbados, Montreal in Canada, La Paz in Mexico, Hertogenbosch in the Netherlands and Singapore.

Messages of sympathy also reached Glasgow from firefighters' representative bodies including the Association of Professional Firemen of Israel and the Queensland Firemen's Association.

Closer to home, there was scarcely a fire service or major city or town in the UK that did not send its own message to Firemaster Chadwick. The list included Lancashire, Kent and Southampton fire brigades and Warwickshire and Caernarvonshire County Councils.

Particularly moving were the handwritten letters from members of the public who had no connection with Glasgow or its Fire Service. For instance Eleanor R Barker (Mrs) of Teignmouth in South Devon said of fire service members, "They risk so much."

Journalists, usually slow to praise, were quick to express gratitude to Martin Chadwick for the assistance he gave the Press during the disaster.

David Eppel, secretary of the Glasgow Branch of the National Union of Journalists, wrote to the Firemaster: "May I offer sincere thanks for your help and co-operation at that most tragic time. Every reporter who was there has spoken highly of the patience you showed in answering our questions in these trying circumstances."

William Lyall, of the Glasgow office of the News Chronicle and Daily Dispatch, wrote: "Even during the worst moments of the Anderston disaster I and all other pressmen were shown the utmost courtesy.

"Without your assistance it would have been impossible for us to do our job and convey to the public something at least of the dangers and sacrifices of the fireman's life."

The most poignant messages of all were exchanged the following morning by the fire stations which had lost personnel: West, South and Central.

Opposite: Four victims of Cheapside Street disaster.

Edward McMillan

John McPherson

George McIntyre

Bill Oliver

FIREMASTER MARTIN CHADWICK

From the darkest days of the Second World War to the dawning of the Swinging Sixties, Martin Chadwick was Firemaster of Glasgow.

Chadwick's extraordinarily long career at the top of his profession began even before taking up his Glasgow post on 1 June 1940 at the age of 39. A native of the North East of England, he began his career in Newcastle-upon-Tyne then held chief officer posts at Kettering, Swansea and Newcastle before moving to Scotland.

Chadwick arrived in Glasgow when the fear of German bombing raids was intense. In January 1941 he announced the recruitment of 4,000 firefighters to assist with the effects of incendiary bombs in particular. Two months later the need for extra firefighters was underlined by the two nights of bombing which devastated neighbouring Clydebank.

Later in 1941 British Fire Brigades were brought under the umbrella of the National Fire Service to improve the service's ability to cope with the Blitz. In July 1941 Chadwick was made Fire Force Commander of the Western No 1 Area which comprised Glasgow and the counties of Lanark, Dumbarton, Stirling and Clackmannan.

While holding this post he was injured in an explosion on board a burning warship, HMS Sussex, on the Clyde. His hands and knees were burned by flying debris.

Chadwick, who was awarded the CBE, argued consistently for better fire safety, particularly the need for the owners of warehouses and other commercial premises to invest in fire alarm systems and other measures.

Chadwick would have seen his worst fears come true at the Cheapside Street Disaster which occurred during his final year as Firemaster. He took charge of firefighting operations which quelled the massive blaze at a bonded warehouse and stopped the spread of fire to other large bonds.

BORN ON CHEAPSIDE DAY

Just six hours before the first fire engines were called out to Cheapside Street, Robert McCleneghen came into the world.

Robert was born at at 13:15 at home in Montrose Street in the Townhead area of Glasgow. He would join the fire service and become a Watch Commander before retiring from Strathclyde Fire & Rescue on the 50th anniversary of the disaster, 28 March 2010.

Robert said: "My mother later told me she knew that the fire was taking place because it was so huge she could see it from the house."

Robert served in two of Scotland's busiest fire stations, Govan and Cowcaddens as well as spells with Staffordshire and Dumfries & Galloway fire and rescue services.

"I always wanted to join the fire service," he added, "and I am very grateful that I've been able to serve my full time while others were not."

Proud firefighter:
Robert McCleneghen

St Mungo in for inspection (above) and out on the Clyde (below).

Two of the vessel's high volume monitors.

THE FIRE BOAT ST MUNGO

In the 1950s and 1960s Glasgow was still a busy port and centre for shipbuilding.

The high concentration of warehouses piled high with inflammable goods made it particularly necessary that Glasgow Fire Service should maintain a fire boat on the River Clyde.

A Marine Division for harbour firefighting was set up in 1942 with two fire boats. One of those boats was withdrawn in 1951 because its timbers had dry and wet rot. The remaining boat continued in service until it was replaced by the St Mungo, named after Glasgow's patron saint.

The Lady Provost, Mrs Myer Galpern, launched the £80,000 St Mungo on 21 May 1959. The occasion was described as a "Red Letter Day" in that year's annual report by the Firemaster, Martin Chadwick. That description would seem a big understatement following the St Mungo's outstanding performance at the Cheapside Street Disaster the following March.

Glasgow Fire Service claimed that the 68ft St Mungo, designed and built by local firms, was the finest firefighting unit of its kind in Britain. Each minute her pumps could draw 32 tons of water from the Clyde and use that water in powerful jets from six monitors.

To deal with oil fires there were foam generators with an output of 350 gallons a minute. There was also a suction apparatus for marine salvage work and two searchlights.

The enormous pumping power of the St Mungo was put to great effect at Cheapside Street. The fire boat was able to feed water to fire pumps through 31 lines of hose, helping not only to quench the blaze at its source but also to stop it spreading to neighbouring warehouses.

There was a strong belief at the time that if Glasgow Fire Service had had to rely solely on the mains water supply, its ability to tackle the blaze would have been much more difficult.

By the mid-1970s Glasgow had declined considerably as a port and centre of shipbuilding. Strathclyde Fire Brigade, which had replaced Glasgow and its neighbouring fire services, saw no further need for a fire boat. In 1978 the St Mungo was sold to an oil industry service company and converted into a workboat. It is believed she was later broken up.

Mrs Dunlop said she had no qualms about her husband joining the fire service. This attitude is shared by Margaret Smith whose husband Joe, was a salvageman who was injured at Cheapside Street when he was almost buried under falling masonry.

Asked if she had been happy for her husband to continue in the Salvage Corps following the Cheapside Street disaster, Mrs Smith said: "Yes. He wouldn't try another career anyway, he's Mr Salvage Corps. After Cheapside Street, every time the fire bell went I wondered would he be back?"

Frank Snoddon was married when he joined Glasgow Fire Service after the Second World War. He says that he and his wife had no concerns about the choice of career and the couple went on to bring up three children in fire service flats.

By contrast, Wallace Branch was persuaded by his wife Jean, a former control officer, to leave Glasgow Fire Service following Cheapside Street.

On the night of Cheapside Street, the pair had been out for a walk when they were passed by four fire engines; at that point they realised something really serious was taking place.

Wallace Branch, who was among the off-duty firemen who turned up for duty, later said: "After Cheapside Street my wife said I had done enough, and I got a security job in a whisky bond."

Children love visiting fire stations, so what must it have been like for children living on the premises?

"To borrow the slogan of Glasgow Prestwick Airport, pure dead brilliant," says Billy Oliver who was one of a large group of 1950s children living in family quarters beside the Glasgow Salvage Corps headquarters in Albion Street.

"Being part of the postwar baby boom, there was a lot of young people from about 50 families," continued Oliver, "It was an easy-going place. We were allowed to play in the yard, things like tig and cowboys and indians, but not football and never on a Sunday."

Smiles for Santa from Salvage Corps children at their Christmas party in the late 1950s.

Discipline was also strict where children were concerned, as Billy Oliver explained: "If you got into trouble you weren't ticked off but your dad would be hauled up in front of the superintendent. Apparently if it was serious enough your dad could have lost his job if he couldn't keep his family under control."

Oliver, his sister Catherine and brother Martin were all born in Albion Street - "We were all Salvage Corps bairns."

The happy life of games in the yard and Christmas parties with gifts from a Salvage Corps Santa came to an end when Oliver's father, Bill, was killed at Cheapside Street. The family could not remain at Albion Street as their flat would be needed by a new salvageman and his family.

The Olivers were found good accommodation, a council flat in a red sandstone tenement in Riddrie. "It was fully carpeted and had a telephone, which for 1960 was really something," added Oliver, who was a nine-year-old at the time of his father's death.

Billy Oliver, who had had to leave his friends from the Salvage Corps, found growing up without a father difficult. His performance at school declined and he could be cheeky with his mum. He did, however, become very close to an uncle who worked in the main fire service control room in Ingram Street.

In 1972 Billy Oliver was about to follow in his father's footsteps and join the Salvage Corps when seven firemen died in a fire at Kilbirnie Street. For his mother's sake he gave up the idea of a fire service career and ended up having a successful one with Strathclyde Police.

Douglas McPherson also remembers having a difficult adolescence after his father, John, a Sub Officer with Glasgow Fire Service, was killed at Cheapside Street.

"I gave my mother a bit of a hard time, but quietened down later when I moved into a flat," said McPherson who ended up as railway system controller with Glasgow Underground.

He too remembers having a happy childhood, living beside the Central Fire Station in Ingram Street: "It was a great place to be a child, and when we escaped from the fire station we'd wander down to the fruit market."

Kay Forsyth also has fond memories of Ingram Street where she was fireman's daughter Kay Robertson. She lived at Ingram Street for ten years until she was 17 in 1963.

"In the winter we'd pile up snowballs and throw them at the firemen when they were running with their sleeves rolled up to get their fire kit." said Forsyth.

Kay Robertson, aged 15, cuddles a cousin in the yard of the Central Fire Station.

On another occasion, when she was about ten, a jet of water pinned her to the wall when a hose practice went wrong - "I had a new dress on and my brother was laughing but I was howling."

Forsyth continued: "We used to play hide and seek on the veranda and I don't know how many times I ran round the corner and found firemen testing their breathing apparatus, and the fright you used to get. And there was a full-sized dummy in a fireman's uniform, and you'd run up and it'd be lying there like a dead body."

One of the larger-than-life members of Glasgow Fire Service was the third-in-command James McIntyre MBE. He was known as the "Goalie" because he used to go to fires wearing a jersey under his fire tunic similar to what a goalkeeper of the day would have worn.

The "Goalie" might have been a tough and respected firemen's fireman who turned out even during his off-duty hours to make sure fires were being fought properly, but to the then Kay Robertson and the other children of Central Station, he was remembered for his tiny Japanese pet dogs.

Tommy McIntyre, who also lived at Ingram Street and whose father George was killed at Cheapside Street, can remember the "Goalie" (who was no relation) letting him walk the dogs - "He was a nice man, Mr McIntyre."

Barbara Shaw spoke of the closeness of the families that lived in a fire brigade block of flats in Lamlash Place in Cranhill - "The children and dogs all were brought up together, I swear it was paradise to live there."

A less happy memory, however, was of her fireman father, Bob McNeill, returning home from Cheapside Street: "Morning had come and my dad was home and we were all hugged like there was no tomorrow. It never left him what he had experienced that night. He was in tears for the men who had died."

CHEAPSIDE STREET TODAY

Fifty years after the wreckage of the Arbuckle, Smith bonded warehouse was cleared away, the site of the Cheapside Street disaster remains a wasteland.

Apart from a derelict-looking building which contains an electricity substation this large area of land is used only as a car park. This scene of apparent neglect is in sharp contrast to neighbouring sites on the north bank of the River Clyde near Glasgow city centre.

Cheapside Street substation.

Glass and aluminium clad offices have sprung up along the Broomielaw and Anderston Quay, forming Glasgow's financial services district. Further west, the Armadillo and the SECC attract hundreds of thousands of people each year to concerts, conferences and exhibitions.

Back at Cheapside Street and Warroch Street, however, the sight of traffic on the Kingston Bridge, opened ten years after the disaster, seems to underline the impression that this is an area that has been leapfrogged by progress. There were firm proposals, before the credit crunch took place, for a mixed development of flats, offices, retail and leisure facilities costing £180 million. At the time of writing, however, these proposals had been put on hold.

View of Kingston Bridge.

Also on the north bank of the Clyde but closer to the city centre, the site of the James Watt Street fire is also vacant and used as a car park. The neighbouring site, to the south at the corner of James Watt Street and the Broomielaw, is occupied by the Scottish Government building, Atlantic Quay.

Left: Blue fire escape door.
Below: James Watt Street exposed factory wall.

The exposed gable wall belonged to the factory where 22 workers died in 1968. Had the fire escape doors on the first and second floors not been padlocked, the workers would have been able to reach the safety of the street via the blue fire escape door (pictured above) in the neighbouring property to the north.

Top: *Graftons fashion store location.*
Middle: *Kilbirnie Street.*
Bottom: *St Andrew's Halls.*

Elsewhere in the city, sites where buildings were destroyed by fire have been transformed. Shoppers walking past the Marks & Spencer store in Argyle Street, for instance, would probably be unaware that the row of shops opposite were built on the site of one of Glasgow's worst fire tragedies - the Graftons fashion store blaze of 1949 which claimed the lives of 13 shop girls.

A less radical transformation took place in Kilbirnie Street where seven firemen were killed in a blaze in the Sher Brothers cash and carry warehouse in 1972. That warehouse was demolished and replaced by one occupying the same site.

The St Andrew's Halls fire of 1962 was a devastating blow to Glasgow's cultural life. Matters could have been much worse had the fire service not controlled the blaze before it could cause irreparable damage to the external walls.

The gutted interior was adapted to house an extension to the Mitchell Library. Today, no-one approaching the library's Granville Street entrance would be able to see any trace of the fire. In fact, stone cleaning has restored it to what would have been its original appearance when it was opened in the late 1870s.

In March 2010, the building was the fitting location for the launch of Tinderbox Heroes at Glasgow's Aye Write! book festival.

The last 50 years has also seen major changes affecting the fire service. Of the 14 fire stations that Glasgow Fire Service operated from in 1960, only one remains operational. That station is Parkhead which is due for replacement. The remaining thirteen were replaced by new build and merger.

Central Fire Station 1900.

New uses have been found for solidly built former fire stations. The engine bay of the old Central Fire Station in Ingram Street plays its part in the Merchant City restaurant scene.

South Fire Station 1916.

Hamish Allan Centre.

Another impressive red sandstone building, the former South Fire Station in Centre Street, houses the Hamish Allan Centre which provides homelessness, counselling and advice services.

Above: North Fire Station 1949.

Left: Flat conversion detail.

Below: North West flat conversion.

The former North and North West fire stations, in St George's Road and Kelbourne Street, respectively, have been converted into flats - all addresses with proud histories.

INVOLVING THE YOUNG

Every year members of Strathclyde Fire & Rescue's Retired Employees' Association and serving members of Strathclyde Fire and Rescue gather at the Necropolis in Glasgow on the anniversaries of the Cheapside Street and Kilbirnie Street fires.

In 2008 the ceremonies at the Cheapside Street Memorial took on a more youthful aspect when the first intake of Strathclyde Fire & Rescue's fire cadet apprentices joined in the proceedings. The cadets, still in their 'teens, lined up smartly alongside the retired and serving members, and on each occasion one of their number presented a wreath to a veteran to lay at the memorial.

The involvement of the cadets at each ceremony reflected a determination within Strathclyde Fire & Rescue that the memory of the sacrifices of previous fire service personnel should not fade.

Also in 2008, the cadets interviewed Cheapside Street veterans as part of a social history project organised by BBC Scotland.

In late 2009, almost all of the cadets moved on to train as firefighters at the Scottish Fire Services College at Gullane in East Lothian. Their places were taken by a new group of young people who were given a big role in events to mark the 50th anniversary of the Cheapside Street disaster.

Opposite: Fire Cadets lined up for wreath laying ceremony.

Left: Retired fireman Jim Miller with cadets, and (above) with fellow Preservation Group members and Anderston Primary pupils.

The cadets joined members of Strathclyde Fire & Rescue Preservation Group to pass on the story of Cheapside Street to pupils of the two primary schools closest to the scene of the disaster, Anderston and St Patrick's primaries.

Pupils from both schools were brought together to design a mosaic commemorating the disaster. For these pupils, the mosaic project and their encounters with veterans of the Tinderbox City era ensured that the story of Cheapside Street was part of their own personal history to remember for the rest of their lives.

Cheapside veteran Felix Lennon meets St Patrick's pupils.
Right: Cheapside memorial ceremony.
Below: Fire Cadets and veterans with BBC staff.

MESSAGE

from Chief Officer Brian Sweeney

When I became Firemaster of what was Strathclyde Fire Brigade in 2004 I promised that our Service would welcome positive change and grasp challenges that would result in a more effective and efficient service for the communities we serve.

Since that time, major changes have taken place. Shortly after my appointment, for instance, we changed our name to Strathclyde Fire & Rescue and my title changed to Chief Officer. This reflected the wider duties, such as water rescue, presented to us by the Fire (Scotland) Act 2005.

To look forward does not mean, however, that you should not look back. I have always taken great pride in the history and traditions of our Service.

Heritage can play a vital role in a modern organisation because past achievements can inspire future success. When I took up my Chief Officer's post I felt it was important to recognise and promote the annual ceremonies to mark the Cheapside Street and Kilbirnie Street fires which claimed the lives of so many firefighters.

I am delighted that the gatherings at both ceremonies at the Necropolis overlooking Glasgow Cathedral have grown year by year, and the ceremony to mark on the 28th of March the 50th anniversary of the Cheapside Street Disaster promises to be a very moving occasion.

The ceremony is only part of the arrangements that have been made to mark that tragic event. This book, Tinderbox Heroes, is another.

Tinderbox Heroes is a tribute to the fire service personnel who protected lives and properties in Glasgow during a very difficult and dangerous period. I am sure that the book will inspire firefighters in Strathclyde and beyond.

I was particularly moved by the tribute given by the then Archbishop of Glasgow, Dr James D Scanlan, at the funeral service for Sub Officer Adrian McGill who died in 1972 sacrificing his life to save a woman trapped in her home: "The example of this brave fireman and his predecessors who have given their lives so unstintingly and unhesitatingly will be an inspiration to us all."

The Tinderbox City era was, in a sense, the bad old days when large numbers of whisky bonds could be sited near the city centre and iron bars be in place on factory windows. Legislation and improved commercial practice now make our communities and buildings safer.

Safety is also a priority for our firefighters who wear helmets and clothing that give much improved protection at fires and other incidents. There is no room for complacency, however, as the Stockline Disaster in 2004 and the terrorist attack on Glasgow Airport in 2007 revealed.

Fire deaths may have fallen considerably over the last ten years and more, but Strathclyde Fire & Rescue is still striving to reduce that number even further. Earlier this year, for instance, a team from Strathclyde Fire & Rescue carried out research on behalf of the Scottish Government into the key causes of fire deaths in the home. This work will be used to drive down fire deaths across Scotland.

Strathclyde Fire & Rescue is also taking a lead in promoting fire sprinklers in homes. This would have as big an impact in improving safety as the introduction of smoke detectors.

Our firefighters - women and men - are now spending a much bigger proportion of their time promoting fire prevention measures such as free home fire safety visits. Of course they remain poised to respond to the next major emergency, as did their predecessors who served and risked their lives in previous generations.

Organisations who lose sight of their history, of where they came from, often lose their way. Through a number of changes in local government Strathclyde Fire & Rescue has never lost its way. For as long as we honour and respect the effort and sacrifices of those who went before us and hold their memory dear... we never will.

Lest we forget.

Brian P Sweeney
Chief Officer

SOME FEATURED PEOPLE

Top (left to right): Bob Aitken, Raymond Ferrari, Felix Lennon and John Jamieson.

Middle: Bob Scouller, Harry Palmer, Vi Aitken and Liz McCreadie.

Bottom: Joe Smith, Allan Reid, John Swanson and Thomas Mundell.

ACKNOWLEDGEMENTS

Tinderbox Heroes is a book that was almost demanding to be published.

Previously, countless books had been written about different aspects of Glasgow's history but none had looked specifically at the events covered in this book.

Glasgow Fire Service had published the excellent Proud Record in 1975 just before the service was absorbed into Strathclyde Fire Brigade. That book, however, covered a much longer period, beginning in the 12th Century, and was printed as a limited edition solely for members of the service.

The approach of the 50th anniversary of the Cheapside Street Disaster highlighted the increasingly pressing need to record the memories of people who had served with Glasgow's fire services during the dramatic postwar period.

It was in 2008 that Brian Sweeney, Chief Officer of Strathclyde Fire & Rescue, proposed the publication of a book to commemorate Cheapside Street, just as four years earlier he had commissioned Everyday Heroes, the book that marked the 30 years of Strathclyde Fire Brigade. Mr Sweeney made his proposal to an invited group of Cheapside Street veterans in Strathclyde Fire & Rescue's headquarters in Hamilton. The proposal was welcomed and many of those veterans now feature in this book.

As co-authors we wish to thank everyone who agreed to be interviewed for Tinderbox Heroes - both former fire service members and family members who can be found quoted in the book along with retired journalist Alex Wattie who covered the Kilbirnie Street fire for the Evening Times. We are also grateful to individuals who preserved fire service records; reports written by fire officers and firemen in the aftermath of Cheapside Street were a vital resource for this book, as were reports by Firemaster Martin Chadwick and his assistant, John Swanson, written after the Graftons fire in 1949. Thanks also to Joe Harkins, co-ordinator of Strathclyde Fire & Rescue Retired Employees' Association, for checking the text, and David Adam, chair of Strathclyde Fire & Rescue Preservation Group and fellow members for assistance in promoting this book and Retired Assistant Chief Officer Neil Turnbull, who played a lead role in initial preparations for the Cheapside Street commemoration

Retired fire control officer Averil McPate gave valuable assistance in contacting veterans and Graeme Kirkwood's website The History of Scottish Fire Brigades **www.btinternet.com/~graeme.kirkwood/index.htm** was also a very valuable source of information.

The moving and dramatic personal stories in Tinderbox Heroes are complemented by equally outstanding photographs. The great majority of these pictures belong to the photographic archive of the Herald & Times Group newspapers. We are extremely grateful to the company, and in particular Tony Carlin, Editor of the Evening Times, for granting us access to the archive which forms such a priceless record of Glasgow's, and Scotland's, history.

Net profits from this book will go to Strathclyde Fire & Rescue's Retired Employees' Association. This organisation is heavily involved in volunteering work, including engaging with young people and spreading the fire safety message.

Alan Forbes   James Smith